Unprecedented:

Building a Multi-Generational Business on Trust, Respect, and the Valuing of People

Chuck Cooper
©2022

Legal Disclaimer

Paperback ISBN: 979-8-9856329-0-3
Digital ISBN: 979-8-9856329-1-0

Unprecedented

Connect with Chuck Cooper

www.chuckcooper.info
http://www.whitewaterconsulting.net
www.linkedin.com/in/chuck-cooper1

WhiteWater Consulting LLC
www.whitewaterconsulting.net
Chuck@WhiteWaterConsulting.net

Unprecedented

Dedication

This book is dedicated to two special groups of people who inspire me every day. First, to you, the entrepreneur and small business owner: thank you for your passion, commitment, and vision to lead your people well. You help make this country the greatest in the world.

I have had the privilege of listening to the stories of how you started your business, the challenges you overcame, and the commitment to lead your people through a common vision and purpose. You are a true inspiration, you have found joy in your journey, and you inspire future entrepreneurs to pursue their dreams. You are my hero.

To my family: I am grateful for the legacy of faith, family, and love that has been passed down from my grandparents, Charles and Jewell Ritcheson, Carl and Ruth Cooper, and my parents, Gary and Pat Cooper. I am grateful to my wife, Debbie, who has been by my side every step of the way as we continue adding to the legacy that was entrusted to us through the raising of our three children, Tyler, Kirsten, and Rachel. What an amazing gift God gave us when He chose us to be your parents. To my grandkids: may this book encourage and inspire you to use your God-given talents, to love people where they are in their journey, and to continue to steward the legacy that will ultimately become yours through the serving of others.

> *"For I know the plans I have for you," declares the Lord, "plans to prosper you and not to harm you, plans to give you hope and a future."*

Jeremiah 29:11 NIV

Acknowledgements

I want to begin by acknowledging and giving thanks to my savior Jesus Christ for saving me in 1992. Without Him, his love, forgiveness, and grace, this book would never have been written.

To those who were directly involved in helping me write this book: I owe a huge debt of gratitude to Kim Thompson-Pinder and her team at RTI Publishing, including Juanita Wootton-Radko. Kim, your book *Author to Authority* and your guidance through the book publishing journey were invaluable as you provided the step-by-step process to keeping myself and the project on schedule from start to finish. I could not have done this without your support and guidance.

I appreciate those of you who continually reached out to offer encouragement, advice, and support throughout the past 15 months as we completed this journey. To Brittney-Nichole Connor-Savarda, Dr. Joey Faucette, Deb Coviello, Kevin Monaghan, Ken Myers, Caryn Lee, and Jon Lingor, thank you. Your friendship is extremely valuable to me, and I am grateful for each of you.

To my good friend, John Smoak, thank you for always encouraging me and for the many prayers you prayed for me during this journey. There were times when I was seeking counsel or needing wisdom, and those were times that God used you in extraordinary ways to provide the words I needed at that moment. I am forever grateful.

To the men who have helped coach, mentor, and offer guidance over the years, I am grateful for the impact you have made in my life. To John Mandeville, John Anthony, John Leake, Leon Tuttle, and David Norman, I am forever indebted to you, and my prayer is that I can use the wisdom you imparted to pay it forward through the serving of others.

To my wife Debbie and our children and their spouses, Tyler and Christy, Kirsten and Erik, and Rachel and Jackson, I am honored and humbled by your interest in this project and the many hours that you sat and listened as I provided updates, insights, and bounced ideas off of you in order to help crystalize my thoughts. This book would not have been possible without your love and support, as I am blessed more than I deserve.

Foreword

Small businesses employ 47.1 percent of the population in the United States, yet an astonishing 50 percent of these small businesses fail after year five. Think about that for a second! That means almost 25 percent of the population in the United States will be unemployed in every five-year cycle. We thus need entrepreneurs to be successful for our economy to flourish, and entrepreneurs need Chuck Cooper's book Unprecedented: Building a Multi-Generational Business on Trust, Respect, and the Valuing of People to be successful.

Most entrepreneurs launch their business because they are passionate about creating something special that will lead to a life of significance and make a difference in the lives of their customers and the communities they are a part of. Yet, the entrepreneur can quickly find themselves in unchartered territory as they try to do everything to keep the business running, which can lead to unexpected surprises and mistakes that can be fatal to their business.

In *Unprecedented*, Chuck shares some real-life stories that owners struggle with, and he walks the reader through the process of how they can overcome the challenges and get their business back on track. These stories are a great reminder that the entrepreneurial journey is not meant to be done alone, as even the best athletes have coaches to help them perform at their best.

Chuck and I share a passion for coaching and working with business leaders. Chuck founded WhiteWater Consulting because he has a passion for mentoring entrepreneurs and serving small and mid-size business owners. He has enjoyed the success of entrepreneurship, and he has also experienced the heartbreak of losing a business because of his poor judgement.

Real-life experiences matter when coaching and mentoring, which is why I appreciate Chuck's commitment to writing *Unprecedented*. He helps business leaders focus on the fundamentals that will give them the best opportunity to win even when competing against much larger companies.

Leadership is essential to being a successful entrepreneur. Your greatest differentiators will be your people and the culture you build, so be intentional about the choices you make. Focus on creating a company that people want to work for and grow with.

Chuck highlights throughout the book the importance of HR and, specifically, HR best practices. Chuck uses his experience and expertise to help the entrepreneur think through the options of how they want their HR infrastructure to be built. This decision-making process may very well have the greatest impact on more businesses than anything else mentioned in this book.

For all of us who have been on the entrepreneurial journey, you understand that there are many challenges we face that require us to make key decisions. These decisions can and often do have an impact on the business performance, which can directly affect our personal lives.

The challenges of attracting and retaining talent, having the financial health to hire that next key person sooner than you expected, or being able to juggle a remote and on-site workforce are some of the more common issues that business owners face today. Will you be ready when the opportunity appears, or would it be beneficial to have a coach or trusted advisor to collaborate with?

As with sports, it's important that we practice the fundamentals regularly to keep our skills sharp. The same is true for small business owners. Practicing and exercising the fundamentals of leadership, communication, and relationship building are necessary to achieve success that is sustainable. Chuck has hit on the key areas that will help you differentiate your company from your competitors and enhance your opportunity to win.

One of my key takeaways from the book is that regardless of whether you are the leader of a startup company or if you are an experienced entrepreneur, the fundamentals of business are the same. The pandemic has changed the world, especially in the way we work, which is why I believe the timing of the book could not be better.

With all of the uncertainty that business leaders face regarding work, their people, and how to best position their company to thrive as the world continues to evolve, this may be the exact time for you to refocus on the fundamentals. *Unprecedented* will help you do exactly that. Leading and communicating with authenticity and transparency will create trust and respect between you and your greatest asset: your people!

Learn and grow,

Matt Doherty;
Former NCAA Basketball Coach, Author and Business Coach

Table of Contents

Unprecedented

Preface

Growing up in a small farming community in central Illinois, as the son and grandson of small business owners, family and our traditions have always been an important part of my life. Every year is a gamble in the life of a farmer as there are significant risks that are out of their control, yet they trust that their process of preparing the soil, planting and cultivating the crop during the growing season, along with timely rainfall and moderate temperatures will provide a harvest that will be used to support their family and the community they live in.

This process showed me that risk and faith were required to be successful.

What I didn't understand was the importance of knowing how to manage risk in my business. In a period of eighteen months, I went from a life of amazing company growth and financial abundance to not having the resources to provide for my family, including buying shoes and clothing for my children.

I went from being a co-owner of a very successful and profitable manufacturing business to plunging deep into debt. I have risen to great heights, crashed to great depths, and risen again by having mentors that coached me personally and professionally, understanding my life's calling, and putting safeguards in my life to hold me accountable.

Those three things did not keep me from making future mistakes, but they did give me the confidence to know that if I stayed true to my personal mission, vision, and values, then I could overcome them.

Our manufacturing company was based in northern Illinois and of the six owners, I was the one who lived in the community and was directly engaged in the business at the day-to-day level. I felt a strong connection to our company, and our company had a strong connection to the local community. We had a great leadership team and wonderful people that worked hard every day and did their best to carry out the mission of our company. This was an opportunity of a lifetime.

However, as can happen when money becomes abundant without having guardrails in your life, greed can rear its head, leading to poor judgment and costly decisions. Greed, along with pride and ego, clouded our thinking as we took money out of the manufacturing business and invested it in what proved to be very risky investments.

The investments failed and we lost all the money we had put into them. In the span of a few months, we went from wealth to facing a mountain of debt that led to the sale of the company to minimize the financial impact to the other shareholders.

I knew I had failed as a leader and, when explaining the situation to my family, I also felt I had failed as a husband, father, and provider. Although there were other owners involved in making the disastrous decisions, I had to own my part of it. I had to accept responsibility for the results of our actions.

As the major employer in a small community, the people in the community viewed and treated me differently. I had lost it all, and placed my family in a very difficult financial position. I give my wife the credit for getting us through the difficult months that followed. She stretched our drastically reduced budget in ways I never would have thought of.

As time passed, I went through the spectrum of emotions: anger, frustration, guilt, and a total loss of confidence. I felt insignificant and defeated, but we pushed forward. We worked through the process of selling the company, moved our family to a new community, and started to rebuild. Our family was able to move on.

It was difficult, but it also gave me the time to really sit and introspect. It was during this time that I was able to gain clarity, understand my life's purpose and passions, and establish the principles that I wanted to live my life by, which led to my ultimate mission: serving, supporting, and helping entrepreneurs and small and mid-size business owners achieve sustainable success.

As time passed, I was able to understand two important concepts. The first was the power of forgiveness. Being forgiven by my family, and then reaching the point where I could forgive myself for my mistakes, set the foundation on which to move forward. Second, like Winston Churchill said, that "Failure is not fatal: it is the courage to continue that counts."

Failure does not define you; however, when you go through difficult times, there are takeaways that can be used throughout the rest of your life. As difficult as the financial debacle was to go through, I am forever grateful for the lessons learned and the personal changes that occurred because of it.

I started White Water Consulting, a human resource (HR) consulting business. The name is inspired by a near miss on some whitewater rapids when I was saved from serious injury by the direct instructions of another canoer with real-life experience and the ability to clearly communicate them. I focused on becoming that guide for others, particularly for entrepreneurs who may not have the experience to avoid the potentially dangerous and expensive "drops in the river" as a small and mid-size business owner.

In this book, I will share my stories, my real-life experience, to help aspiring entrepreneurs navigate the post-COVID-19 business landscape. This includes insights on the evolution of business leadership, communication within the workplace, the new generations of workers, the "isms" of workplace culture, and best HR practices, such as outsourcing and compliance.

Entrepreneurs were already facing a growing field of challenges before the pandemic and having the guidance of a mentor can make a world of difference.

Success can be exhilarating. Once you have climbed to the top of the mountain, the view is breathtaking. However, not much grows at the top, so it can be hard to sustain ourselves while there. Mistakes are a part of life, and we all have our moments when we fall. Descending from the peak is not the end of the world because it is in the valleys where we grow and cultivate our resources. Armed with greater wisdom, enhanced supplies, and the right guidance, the next climb can be even better. So, join me as we climb to the peak together.

Unprecedented

Chapter 1: Introduction

"Human resources isn't a thing we do.
It's the thing that runs our business."
Steve Wynn

Over the years, I have had the opportunity to work with entrepreneurs whose businesses have experienced great success both at launch and in the long term. I have also worked with those whose businesses have faltered and failed within the first year. The most heartbreaking ones are those that launch with great momentum and experience initial success, but then collapse in on themselves, all too often because they did not have good HR practices, policies, or processes in place to support their growth.

A few years ago, I had a prospective client that was a high-flying technology company enjoying great success. The leadership team was made up of talented, experienced executives with a well thought out go-to-market strategy and who had raised tens of millions of dollars in funding. After launch, they enjoyed sales growth that was off the charts, while also opening new markets in multiple states. Everywhere they turned, they found success. In less than fifteen months, the company grew from twelve employees to 250 and had offices in seventeen states.

The trouble was that the management team was focused solely on one side of the equation: revenue and expansion. They refused to hire an internal HR team or even consider HR outsourcing. They were hiring in large numbers and at great velocity. Without a solid HR infrastructure in place, however, they were not able to ensure that the market managers they were hiring had all the necessary skills and training to support the company's growth and properly oversee all the salespeople and other employees.

Inconsistencies in hiring, firing, and promoting practices began to generate frustrations among the company's employees. Employee benefits were being mismanaged, causing many people to miss important deadlines, which led to further complications or outright loss of their benefits. Some people were being overpaid; others were being underpaid. All of this generated dissatisfaction among the employees.

As the rapid expansion started to become unwieldy, the revenues began to plateau and the expenses grew. They were forced to start retracting their expansion and laying off increasingly larger swaths of their workforce, at times as many as seventy at once. Within two years, they went from 250 employees down to twenty-five. The layoffs made people feel that they were being misled and treated unfairly, leading them to file complaints with the Equal Employment Opportunity Commission (EEOC).

This led to fines that burned through even more of their capital. Essentially, they were a company that experienced great success out of the gate, only to completely collapse in on themselves because they did not have the necessary HR infrastructure in place.

Being proactive and implementing HR best practices (including manager training, personnel policies, and hiring processes) could have prevented the collapse. The mistakes made by leadership not only impacted their company, but also the lives of their employees, families, customers, and vendors. With leadership comes the burden of command and the responsibility for the consequences.

If you are reading this book and do not know a lot about HR, then check out this article about three HR basics for small business owners:
https://whitewaterconsulting.net/3-hr-basics-for-small-business-owners/.

Times Have Changed

Leadership in business has always been challenging, and in recent years, the changing demographics of generations in the workforce has shifted and reshaped those challenges. The era of CEOs operating in isolation and separated from their workers by layers of hierarchy has been forced to move towards a flattening of the organizational chart, thus becoming more collaborative, empathetic, and focusing on transparency and more direct communication.

The notion of the employee being in service to the company has been pushed aside in favor of an approach focused on how the company can support, empower, and develop their workers. The primary focus is no longer solely on profit, but also to incorporate an awareness of how companies and products impact people, the community, and the global environment. How leaders balance their commitment to these areas and maintain profitability is a significant challenge, as a company's ability to generate profits is still necessary to fund these new initiatives.

Additionally, each generation of workers not only approach their work in different ways, but they also have very diverse approaches to how they live their lives. Paradigms are shifting and overlapping. As such, leaders and managers need to understand and support multiple perspectives and needs at the same time.

The baby boomers and those of a similar age, who are quickly approaching retirement, have operated under a particular mindset for their entire lives: go to college, find a job, stick with that job for the long haul, work hard, and the reward is increased compensation and career advancement. Job turnover was markedly low for their generation. They stayed at the same job, knowing that the benefits would allow them to retire comfortably and that their healthcare would be covered and not drain their retirement funds.

Millennials and Generation Z workers are much more focused on a work–life balance. They have seen the results of previous generations' pursuit of corporate success and technological advancement at the expense of people. They have seen the employee burnout, failed marriages, broken families, growing mental health challenges, destruction of the environment, social injustice, political extremism, and a wider financial divide than ever before, just to name a few issues.

Younger generations are now focused on living their lives and are much more disposed to align themselves with terms like purpose, development, empowerment, and coaching. They are often more interested in making lateral career moves rather than a constant upward climb. The majority of millennials and Gen Zers want employee benefits with healthcare coverage that offers high deductible plans, as they have a lower monthly premium and (in some cases) qualify for a Health Savings Account, which can be used for future medical costs, offer tax advantages, and can be rolled over from year to year. Offering benefits that focus on mental health services and student loan assistance are beneficial when it comes to attracting and retaining younger employees.

The pandemic has further upended the landscape. When COVID-19 hit, only 40 percent of companies in the United States had policies and procedures in place for employees to work remotely. Suddenly, they were forced to be 100 percent remote effective immediately. This generated a lot of unexpected questions within organizations, which included:

- What tools do workers need to work effectively from home?
- What is the company responsible for, and what are the individual employees responsible for?
- How do we protect private and sensitive data?
- How do we build and maintain a community within our workforce when everyone is separate and remote?

- As we return to our original workspaces, are we requiring our employees to come back to the office or giving them an option?
- How many can continue to work remotely?
- How do we keep our workspaces sanitized and safe?
- Do we require vaccination?

Having proper and effective HR infrastructure and policies are crucial to navigating these challenges.

The Great Resignation

COVID-19 has given people the time to contemplate and assess how they are living their lives and to determine what is most important to them. This is leading to the desire to make significant adjustments to their personal and professional life, including who they are willing to work for.

Throughout the pandemic, many of us have taken the time to reflect on our lives, as we have been forced to recognize that we are not immortal. This virus does not differentiate based on sex, age, job title, socioeconomics, or geography. We are all at risk, and our lives could be permanently changed in an instant. This revelation has made many rethink what they want out of their employment.

This period has also been extremely stressful for married couples and families as they had to adapt to not only working from home, but also working with their kids to ensure that they received the online learning they needed.

As the option to return to conventional offices and workspaces returns, some employees will want to continue working remotely while others need the social interaction with teammates and management to feel connected and fulfilled.

Based on our conversations with clients and their employees, there is a chasm of perspectives and approaches between the older and younger generations. Older generations are more likely to be content with working from an office location, whereas many in the younger generations prefer the flexibility of working remotely, yet they still desire to be a part of a community and maintain personal connections.

I believe that most companies will seek to offer a hybrid work model going forward, with the understanding that the effectiveness of this new model will be based on productivity and the impact on the company culture, including employee morale. Businesses of all sizes have no choice but to become agile and adapt to the ongoing evolution of the workplace or lose a significant number of employees to other workplaces that do. For those in HR departments, this includes auditing, adapting, and updating their policies and procedures.

Prior to the pandemic, we found that companies frequently failed to keep up with the changes in employment regulations. There have been many instances where I asked for a copy of the company's handbook, and then had to wait while they searched to find it, all too often covered in dust. This was not an example of using best practices or being proactive.

Ensuring that company policies comply with state and federal laws is crucial for the well-being of a business and its employees. During the pandemic, there were an incredible number of laws passed that pertained to the Equal Employment Opportunity Commission (EEOC), *Fair Labor Standards Act* (FLSA), unemployment, essential versus non-essential employee guidelines, plus other programs including Paycheck Protection Program (PPP) loans, *Families First Coronavirus Response Act* (FFCRA), and Employee Retention Credit (ERC). Policies and processes need to be constantly monitored and updated, and compliance should be a part of every review.

Product and market strategy alone are not enough to guarantee success. Generating revenue is not enough to ensure a company's survival. The employees at all levels are the vital cogs that enable the machine to function, and the HR policies and procedures of the company are what determine their ability to function, for good or for ill. In this book, we are going to examine the key ways that HR infrastructure helps to ensure success, productivity, and longevity in businesses of all sizes.

What This Book Covers

I want to give small businesses the foundation and tools that they need to create a successful and adaptable HR infrastructure by looking at the roles of leadership, company culture, communication, compliance, and HR best practices throughout this book.

Let's start with a quick overview of each one.

Leadership

Effective leadership is critical to developing a healthy organization. The leaders of a business are responsible for designing and defining its mission, vision, values, as well as the company's culture. For small and mid-size businesses to succeed, everyone in the organization needs to be working in sync with one another towards a common goal. This makes communication and staff development crucial for the performance and future health of the company.

Company Culture

A company's greatest asset is its people. The company culture is the commonly held values and principles that shape the behavior of your people, including what they say, what they do, and how they make their customers and vendors feel. You can see the difference in culture when you walk into a Ritz-Carlton hotel versus any other hotel chain.

Do you want a good company culture or a world-class culture? The most successful companies recognize the importance of culture; they focus on it, train for it, and live and breathe it every day. An organization's culture is a key differentiator when it comes to attracting and retaining high-performing employees and to company's long-term success.

Communication

Communication is important for everyone from the CEO to the newest employee. It is the key to fostering good working relationships, improving morale, and increasing efficiency. Communication is not just about speaking; it is also listening with the intent to understand before being understood.

Open and authentic communication from leadership establishes trust and respect, which refines and improves internal relationships, thus leading to a positive culture and enhanced level of employee engagement.

Communication methods can vary depending on whether you are in person or remote, and can range from being respectful with your team's time by keeping meetings short and on topic (so they can meet their deadlines) to using Slack or IM to check in with those working remotely and responding quickly if you get a message from them.

Compliance

This topic is not sexy and does not offer much sizzle; however, it is critically important. Compliance helps an organization mitigate risks as it relates to being an employer. Companies that are proactive with compliance are typically more buttoned up throughout the company, which adds to its stability, sustainability, and financial value.

HR Best Practices

When a company implements HR best practices, it has an impact on the company culture, the level of employee satisfaction, and engagement. A company can acquire these best practices by building up an internal HR team over time, or leadership can elect to outsource HR to a provider that offers a plug-and-play system that delivers best practices immediately.

When looking at the five themes of this book, you will see that they are all interconnected. Indeed, the most successful companies score high in all these areas.

I want to invite you to join me on an exploration of what HR means in your business. Many companies see it as an unnecessary expense, but I have learned that HR is the foundation that allows you to grow successfully and maintain that growth for many years to come—and this book will show you how.

As we start this journey, I would love to offer you a free online assessment of where your business is at HR-wise. To take this assessment, visit www.chuckcooper.info. Are you ready to take your business to the next level? Then turn the page.

Key Takeaways

- Implement HR basics early.

- Incorporate HR into the company growth strategy to ensure that growth doesn't implode in on itself.

- Leaders need to become more agile and adapt as the world of work evolves.

- Committing to high-caliber leadership, culture, communication, compliance, and HR leads to an organization that your people will want to be a part of.

- How well does your company score? Take the 10-question assessment by clicking here: www.chuckcooper.info.

Chapter 2: How Business Leadership Needs to Change

"The best leaders don't know just one style of leadership—they're skilled at several and have the flexibility to switch between styles as the circumstances dictate."
Daniel Goleman

Mason sat at the head table, looked at all his employees, and sighed to himself. He had successfully led his company for forty-five years, but now for the first time, he felt lost. COVID-19 had hit his business hard, and at sixty-three, trying to navigate all the necessary changes had taken its toll.

One of the reasons for this meeting was the recent company-wide poll that showed employee satisfaction at work was at an all-time low, and that shocked him. He thought that he had done well for his employees. Now, however, he realized that he did not understand what they needed, and he wanted to change that.

The next few hours were an eye-opener for Mason. He saw older, faithful employees no longer feeling valued. One employee said he felt like he was being manipulated to retire early and get him out of the way. Younger employees complained that everything was structured to keep the baby boomers happy, and that the company did not care about them at all.

"What a mess," Mason thought to himself, but he knew that he had to do something, or he may not have a company five years down the road.

He stood up and tried to make eye contact with everyone in the room and to the camera for those who were working from home.

"First, I want to tell you that I do not have all the answers yet, but I have heard each and every one of you and have taken extensive notes to prove it," he said while he held up pages of written paper. "I am making a commitment to you right now that within the next year all of these will be explored, and changes will be made that will benefit everyone in this company."

Mason was not sure how he was going to do all of this, but he would make it happen.

The next day, he met with a good friend and fellow CEO for lunch. He told him what had happened, and his friend said something that finally gave him hope. "Mason, I know that you have put off starting an HR department, but now is the time. Many of the complaints your employees have could easily be handled if you had HR best practices in place. I knew that it was time for me to do it, and I found a great company that I outsource it to and it has made all the difference in my business."

Mason took his advice and over the next eighteen months, made the changes needed. Two years into the process, employee satisfaction was through the roof and so were the profits!

Many Changes

Over the last twenty to thirty years, we have seen changes in almost every aspect of our lives. From technology and economics to social and cultural norms, the work we are doing has changed as have the methods we use, not to mention the demographics of those doing the work. Although many of our business policies, processes, and systems have changed, the way we manage our people has not.

The Industrial Revolution upended our previous agriculture-focused existence, driving it to a primarily manufacturing workforce supporting a consumer product lifestyle. Business structures and leadership styles shifted to a factories-and-assembly-lines model, which fueled the economic growth and booms that followed.

That is, however, where most business models have remained. The vast majority of companies are still operating under a pyramid-shaped hierarchical approach, with owners and top executives issuing directives to an increasingly further removed workforce. Simply because it was a successful model decades ago, does not mean it is the right model for our current time and circumstances.

The same is also true with leadership. Just because a person was a good leader twenty years ago, does not mean that they are the right leader today to help the company achieve its future mission and vision. Leaders need to be able to adapt, grow, and change regardless of the size of their company.

Growth in technology has led to increased productivity and operational efficiency, thus generating decades of prosperity. However, leadership within small and mid-size companies has been fixated on the growth and profitability of the organization and on being accountable to the shareholders. The driving focus has been on profit above all, and the push has been towards maximizing productivity to the near exclusion of everything else.

Unfortunately, this has caused many in leadership to begin viewing their people as a line item on a financial statement instead of as valuable assets responsible for generating the revenue and growth of the company. A company's greatest asset is its people.

These are not only the problems of large multinational corporate entities. They affect small and mid-size companies as well, impacting significant numbers of workers. According to the Small Business Administration and Bureau of Labor Statistics, as of 2021, there are 31.7 million small businesses in the U.S., and they employ approximately 60.1 million people, which represents 47.1 percent of the U.S. private workforce.

Post-World War II and Hierarchy-Style Leadership

After World War II, the U.S. transformed from an inward-looking, isolated country into an international economic powerhouse. The transition from the general store with only a few employees and where most people lived and worked within their community, to the society-changing boom of manufacturing required businesses to look at management structures differently.

Most small businesses had a small list of tasks that needed to be completed, and their employees did not require any specialized education or training. As manufacturing became the dominant model, the lists of tasks grew exponentially, requiring much larger numbers of people to complete them. For the sake of efficiency, workers were trained for and assigned to only one specific section of the assembly line, doing the same task repeatedly every day.

As companies grew and began operating in multiple locations, including different states and countries, the size and complexity of their workforces expanded further and they were forced to create separate departments to oversee different aspects of the business, such as sales, marketing, inventory, manufacturing, and management.

Early on, the offices for those in management were most often located in close proximity to the operations, and the chain of command was very short. Oversight was relatively immediate, and the connection between owners and workers was direct.

As companies succeeded and the economy boomed, businesses continued to grow, adding more employees and expanding their infrastructure. As the organizations enlarged, so too did the distance between the average employee and the C-Suite or executive managers, such as Chief Executive Officer (CEO), Chief Financial Officer (CFO), and Chief Operating Officer (COO).

The relationship between management and the workforce became more hierarchical, employing a top-down, pyramid-shaped structure with a narrow center of power at the top trickling down over a widening base of subordinate levels. Within the hierarchy leadership model, managers are responsible for their teams. When the primary focus of company expectations is maximizing profitability, though, managers' relationships to their teams tend to become purely professional. Anything personal is off the table, and they often use a one-size-fits-all approach for every situation.

Employees worked at the same time every day, took their breaks at the same time, and quitting time was the same as well. There were opportunities for advancement, but they were limited. Everyone was gauged by the same parameters during their annual review, and given merit increases if they had jumped through enough hoops in the year. The prevailing attitude was that any employee was easy to replace. This perceived expendability played a major part in shaping the view of employees as tools rather than assets.

One of the major challenges that businesses face today is the lack of trust that has grown between employees and employers. The hierarchical lack of connection and communication has not only led to a breakdown in trust, but also to a decrease in the capacity for understanding why that breakdown has occurred and what, if anything, can be done to resolve it.

The Problems COVID-19 Created

Quite simply, COVID-19 changed everything for people, especially their relationship to their work. Suddenly, we were being told to shelter in place, cut off from our friends and families. Large swaths of the population were unable to work because the businesses employing them had been ordered to close, leading to enormous amounts of anxiety and stress over how to support themselves.

Individuals working in healthcare and other essential industries were faced with the stressful task of doing their jobs without clear guidance on safety precautions. In addition, their jobs were made increasingly difficult due to high resistance to protective measures of any kind.

Those able to work remotely were faced with the challenge of transforming their homes not only into functioning office spaces, but also, for those with children, into virtual classrooms. Many who were unable to work on-site or remotely turned to online entrepreneurship to try to make ends meet.

The personal, social, employment, and economical challenges and problems caused by the sudden global pandemic are too numerous to list, but when it comes to the difficulties faced by business leaders and managers, they can be broken down into five main categories.

1. Lack of Control. There was nothing leadership could do to reduce the impact of the virus. The C-Suite and business owners were left feeling unsure about their future and the future of their companies as they were suddenly confronted with unexpected and powerful forces completely outside of their control.

2. No Predictable Timeframe. They never anticipated a virus could or would shut down the entire world all at one time. As well, many in leadership were expecting the pandemic to run its course within a few months, after which everything would promptly get back to normal.

3. Unsure What to Do: Companies had to move from a centralized location to a fully remote or decentralized workforce and it caught leadership flat-footed, leaving many unable to move their company forward. At the outset of the pandemic, only 40 percent of companies had policies and procedures in place to accommodate and support remote work.

4. Concern for Personal Well-Being. Leaders were worried for their own families as well as the lives of their employees and their families.

5. Concern for Company Survival. I remember calling and checking in with business owners to see if there was anything I could do to help. With most offices being closed, I wound up leaving voicemails, but was surprised at the number of people who returned my call seeking ideas and input on their options.

Late one evening my phone rang, and the business owner said, "I am glad you called as I need help. I am sitting in my office after 9:00 at night, scared to death that I am about to lose my business. I am greatly concerned about my employees and their families, but I am most concerned for my spouse and kids, as they have no idea how much their world is about to change."

I was able to help him reduce his anxiety that evening and scheduled a meeting for the following day. We worked through the process of qualifying them for a PPP loan, and within a couple of weeks, they were able to get funding to support them through the next four months. With that pressure relieved, they were able to make further decisions and changes to help the company move ahead and are thriving today.

The Evolution of Remote Working

Aside from the challenges and anxieties, the pandemic has also given people time to assess their lives, and to examine what has been working well and what has not. This included reflecting on their priorities and reconnecting with the things that were most important to them. Prior to the pandemic, we heard people saying that they were searching for a work–life balance and were stressed because society had glorified the person who was always on 24/7 and 100 percent committed to their job. This was the dedicated worker who felt the need to respond to every email or voicemail regardless of day or time, and who refused to take paid time off (PTO) lest they be looked upon negatively.

Over the past several decades, corporate leadership has rewarded these efforts and set them as the standard for what a rockstar employee should be. In fact, this was an unhealthy standard against which all were measured.

After a client company meeting, I had a National Vice-President of Sales say to me, "The individuals in this room are our thoroughbreds and we are going to ride them until they fall over, as we push to maximize our sales production and profitability." This created a short-term win for the company, but was a long-term disaster as their team left one by one for new opportunities or they burned out. As Chris Allen, the founder of Always About People, says, "Love people, use things…the other way around never works!"

As the first month, then two, of the pandemic passed, we started seeing people making the adjustment to working from home. They remained very productive and, in many situations, were even more productive. Studies have shown that productivity increased during the pandemic, that employees worked more hours than when they were in the office, and that they were happier. People began settling into their new routines and recognized that remote work had its advantages.

There was no commuting to and from the office, and no travel to client or sales meetings. People also began dressing more casually, and their work environment became more relaxed. With less internal meetings and micro-management, employees began building their new daily schedules based on what fit best for them, mixing blocks of work with their personal lives instead of against them.

It became commonplace for kids or pets to "drop in" on virtual meetings, to the point that it was essentially expected and even anticipated as an added heartwarming bonus feature. People began to realize they did not have to be on 24/7 to complete their work, and they could have a more balanced life.

As we started to gain a firmer grasp on the pandemic, and cities, states, and countries worked to reopen, many employers began requiring their employees to come back to the office, only to find that many in the workforce wanted to remain working remotely, generating tension between management and employees. The world of being an employer had changed.

Chris Dyer, author of the book, *Remote Work*, said, "I believe the pandemic has taken many of the concepts of how we approach working and pulled them forward by at least five years. This means the way CEOs and business owners lead will have to change for them to retain a connection to their employees and for their company to remain relevant." You can listen to the podcast episode here: https://lnns.co/9s75WO-vMm_

Collaborative-Style Leadership

By all appearances, we are on the cusp of another revolution wherein companies are forced to rethink their purpose and approach. A few years ago, Larry Fink, CEO of BlackRock Investments, spoke on CNBC about the rising importance of environmental, social, and governance (ESG) investing. You can check out Larry Fink's 2018 letter to CEOs here: https://www.minterellison.com/articles/blackrock-annual-letter-to-ceos-2018.

One of the impacts of the past year is the rising awareness of the social component. We are having more discussions on topics such as mental health, race, gender and diversity, employee engagement, human rights, labor standards, and data protection. Employees, customers, and the marketplace are all becoming more vocal about how companies' operations impact society and the environment. As these discussions continue to evolve, they will shape the decisions that leaders make about how they operate their businesses.

As I have spoken with business owners and leadership teams over recent years, I began doing deeper dives into whether they were a part of any peer-to-peer advisory groups or had any form of community around them to serve as a board of directors. What I learned was that leaders who were a part of a peer group or had a community around them were able to make decisions more quickly and with greater confidence. They were able to keep their teams focused by providing consistent communications, which kept their teams engaged and motivated, knowing that everyone was working toward a common goal or vision, and led many of these companies to thrive despite COVID-19 or social and political unrest.

Collaborative-style leadership, which is a flattening or delayering of the hierarchy model, has become the key. It is built on the four Cs of leadership: Communication, Connection, Commitment, and Care. I would also add one additional C to include remaining Curious. Although the decision-making is still centralized to the C-Suite or owner level, the process by which information is gathered allows for input from a variety of perspectives to be voiced and considered prior to a decision being made. If employees are valued, seen, and heard, then relationships can be restored and the company culture can be enhanced.

With collaborative-style leadership, the manager becomes one of the most important positions within the company. They are the conduit for bringing the mission and values of the company to the frontline workers. Managing is done on a one-to-one model, generating a deeper relationship between the manager and the employee. The manager becomes a coach to their team members, helping to motivate and challenge them towards becoming the best versions of themselves.

To be successful, a manager needs to get to know the team members personally and professionally, seeking to develop a deeper, more personal relationship with them. This requires the manager to be agile and adaptable, as each team member may have a very different set of needs. This style of management leads to happier, healthier, and more fulfilled employees, which then improves and strengthens the company's culture and performance.

The internal communication model has changed. Rather than a top-down approach, there is now a vocal demand for open lanes of communication flowing in both directions. Employees want the ability to bring issues (and potential solutions) to the attention of their managers or the owner levels directly.

When a frontline worker recognizes a problem in the production process and can bring the issue to their manager to discuss a solution or, if needed, to advance the issue to upper management, this generates a collaborative approach to problem solving, thus offering the best chance at finding optimal solutions. This style of communication brings everyone in the organization together and creates a team environment, which encourages a singular focus on accomplishing the company mission.

Another important aspect of collaborative-style leadership is inclusivity. Traditionally, white men have made up most corporate boards, C-Suites, and management positions. As we look forward, having diversity in leadership is vital if a company is to remain relevant. Including different perspectives, genders, and ethnicities will help companies implement new policies, processes, and ways of thinking, which will be necessary to remain not only relevant, but also successful.

It is important to understand that this style of leadership will not be accepted by everyone, and the hierarchy-style leadership will remain important for institutions like the military and healthcare. For most small and mid-size businesses, however, it will become imperative for leaders to become more agile and strengthen their level of emotional intelligence. They will need to develop the qualities of empathy, trust, authenticity, and transparency. In fact, these qualities will become increasingly important as millennials and Gen Zers have more of a presence in the workforce and start to assume leadership positions.

Moving Forward

Leaders of the present and future will be best suited by putting ego aside and becoming more human to their teams. The way they communicate with their teams is crucial if their desire is to build trusting relationships with everyone in the company.

This may mean admitting to having made mistakes or not having all the answers. By strengthening their relationships with their workers, though, they will build trust and respect, enhancing employee engagement, personal fulfillment, and a healthier workforce, which will lead to higher productivity and greater financial performance.

One of the challenges that companies will be confronted with is the potential skills gap between current managers and the new sets of skills needed to lead an evolving workforce effectively. Ensuring your managers are armed and prepared may require an investment of additional training and resources.

Companies will want to consider having smaller teams and minimizing the administrative-related tasks that managers are currently used to, so they can have more time to work directly with their teams. To be successful, managers must become good listeners, be capable of asking questions to engage their team members, and be willing to be transparent with their teams.

They will need to provide opportunities for regular feedback, both positive comments and any necessary difficult conversations. We all need consistent feedback so we can have clarity on how we are performing. How often have you asked yourself: *How am I doing? Am I in danger of losing my job?* The more we ask ourselves these types of questions without any answers or feedback, the more anxious we become. Creating a rhythm of regular feedback minimizes those internal stresses and provides your team with the clarity and confidence to perform at their best.

Over the years, leadership development has frequently been outsourced to consultants or outside training companies and has not generated the desired results. It is critically important to have your entire organization operating together, following company values to accomplish the intended mission. This can only happen when all your managers and their teams are operating with the same values, processes, and methods.

The CEO and business owner will always be responsible for setting the mission, vision, and values of the company, but they are also responsible for leadership development. This requires being personally involved in the company training when new employees are brought onboard, especially managers, and leading the corporate culture by example. Whether your company has a good culture or a world-class culture depends on *you*.

Key Takeaways

- Communication is the key to building trust and having people feel valued.

- Those who managed people prior to COVID-19 may need additional training on developing people skills in order to be effective going forward.

- Managers must provide ongoing feedback to their team. Having many little conversations over time can lead to big results.

- To learn more about leading through a crisis, visit: www.whitewaterconsulting.net/managing-during-crisis

Chapter 3: Understanding the Needs of Each Generation

"We need to remember across generations that there is as much to learn as there is to teach."
Gloria Steinem

In a polarized world, everything gets divided into an "us" versus "them" paradigm, and the same can wind up being true in business, especially when there are multiple generations working together. Different generations in the workplace can mean more opportunities for success, but it can also mean more challenges, depending on how the company leadership deals with the generational differences.

Creating an environment where each individual feels valued is paramount to a business and the level of success it achieves. Leadership who understands this and executes a strategy that pulls the best of each generation together, fitting it into the mission of the organization, will become an employer of choice in the marketplace. They will become a destination for high-caliber talent, and the organization will have a world-class culture, creating raving fans among employees, customers, and vendors alike.

To create an environment where each generation feels valued, you must first understand some of the common perspectives and approaches of each generation, and then seek out the common ground between them. Each generation can add value to the collective team if given the opportunity. From knowledge and wisdom gained through real-life experience to the understanding of technology to the strength and energy of a younger generation, everyone brings value to the team.

Each generation sees the world through the lens of their experiences growing up. Although there were significant differences between the worlds of the baby boomers, Generation X, millennials, and Generation Z, each generation has a preference regarding methods for learning, receiving communication, what work means to them, and the values around which they choose to live their lives.

One size does not, in fact, fit all. Whether we are talking about approaches to managing employees, communication, or handling employee benefits, modern leaders must be fluent in the various needs of different generations and be adaptable and constantly evolving in their perspectives and approaches in order to meet them.

For a contrasting example, as a recruit in the military, your first destination is boot camp, where you focus on learning the traditions, tactics, and methods of being a soldier. You learn how to work as a member of a team to accomplish tasks. It does not matter what generation you are a part of. The goal is to meld everyone together into a team that accomplishes their mission as a single unit.

Obviously, the environment of small and mid-size businesses is not the same as the military, but our goal is also to work together as a team, put aside our individual differences, and achieve a common objective. It is important for a leader to know how to bring people together as a team yet manage them as individuals, so they can bring the best version of themselves to work every day.

We now have multiple generations in the workforce, and everybody has different sets of needs. Having a clear general understanding of the different generations is essential, but it is also important to remember the dangers of painting with a broad brush. Whatever generation they are a part of, people are individuals, all with unique and different skills, personalities, and preferences. Building a culture that is focused on meeting the needs of your people will require both a general understanding and direct personal engagement.

Baby Boomers

"Baby boomer" refers to the boom of births that took place after the end of World War II, between 1946 and 1964. Prior to the millennials, they were the largest generation in history and now many of them are transitioning into retirement. One of the greatest challenges they are facing, however, is establishing adequate funding for that retirement.

Some baby boomers have been forced into retirement earlier than expected due to ageism, whether they financially can afford it or not, and are forced to take part-time work to generate further income. Others who have the option to remain in place are holding on to their corporate positions much further into their typical retirement years.

In either case, a primary concern for working baby boomers is job stability. They want to know that they will be able continue earning enough income to support their retirement as they draw closer to the end of their working years. In terms of benefits, they want a healthcare plan with a low deductible, so if something major happens health-wise, they do not have to dip into their retirement funds to pay the bills.

Generation X

This generation is made up of those who were born between the mid-1960s and early 1980s. Many Gen X'ers are finding themselves to be part of the "sandwich generation," as they chose to have kids later in life and are also supporting their aging parents who are living longer. They understand the methods and approaches of the baby boomers because it was part of how they grew up, but they were also there for the beginnings of digital technology.

Many in this generation were heavily impacted by the dotcom bust in the early 2000s and the financial crisis of 2008. They are in their prime earning years, so career advancement and compensation are top of mind for them. However, they are also seeking the proverbial work–life balance as they try to care for their kids, care for their parents, juggle their household finances, and have time for outside interests. They view employee benefits such as retirement plans, health insurance, dental, vision, life, and disability insurance as being of high importance.

Gen X'ers tend to excel at working autonomously, accept responsibilities, need little supervision, and finish tasks within deadlines. They thrive when given opportunities to work with new technology, and appreciate concise and direct communication. This generation of employees often finds remote work attractive, and employers should offer more flexibility in this regard to retain them, or they will be at risk of losing them to a competitor.

Millennials

There were approximately 72.26 million millennials born between 1981 and 1996. Just entering the workforce during the dotcom bust and the following recession, many millennials struggled to find employment on top of being weighted down with student loan debt. They were raised during the digital age, so they interact differently with their co-workers. They prefer texting as their primary form of communication and utilize social media to engage with others. They want experiences, not a 9–5 job, and they want to feel valued and recognized for the talents they bring to the organization.

For Baby Boomers and Gen Xers, job security and advancements are top priorities and there is an unspoken commitment of loyalty to the company for future service, advancement, and higher income.

Millennials bring a very different perspective, as they are focused on the corporate purpose, including the mission, vision, and values of the company and how their job relates to it. They want to know the "why" behind management decisions, how the work they do ties into achieving the corporate mission, and that their work is having a positive impact on their community and society.

Many have already started their families, with kids that are in elementary or middle school, and are looking ahead at paying for college while starting to lay the foundation for retirement savings. Thus, they want the flexibility to look at the different medical plan options and pick one that is the best fit for them, their family, and their plans.

Although this generation often receives criticism from older generations and those in media, they bring a much-needed change to the workforce that will impact the way businesses function. They are great students and become more engaged when given opportunities to learn and develop their skills. This generation is the driving force behind the company and culture disruption, which will lead to additional changes regarding the future of work.

Generation Z

The 67.06 million people born between 1997 and 2012 are referred to as Generation Z, and appear to be more adaptable than members of other generations. Growing up during a recession and seeing their parents struggle to make ends meet pushed Gen Z'ers to take control of their finances and do more with less: two strengths that can translate to creativity, innovation, and versatility on the job.

The intense polarization of the socio-economic and political environment in which they grew up has made them generally more tolerant and inclusive, more open to multiple perspectives, and willing to speak their own minds. Members of Generation Z also tend to stay on task without constant oversight from management.

Gen Z'ers are less likely than millennials to trust companies, but they can be swayed. The needs of Generation Z employees include work–life balance and well-being, meaning they value employee benefits such as mental health, paid time off, and activities that create a sense of community.

As most of them are dealing with student loans, they would rather have an employer offer a range of benefit plans from the low deductible, low out-of-pocket costs to the high deductible that has a low premium. Since they are likely only going to the doctor if something major happens to them, they want to pay less for their benefits coverage in the day-to-day sense. They would rather establish a health savings account as part of their healthcare plan to help pay for possible medical expenses in the future.

To win over this generation, companies need to highlight their efforts at being good global citizens, as actions speak louder than words. The three areas that Generation Z is looking for corporate America to address are sustainability, climate change, and world hunger. According to a report published by Deloitte, in order for employers to attract Gen Z'ers, they must be ready to adopt a speed of evolution that matches the external environment.

This includes developing robust training and leadership programs with a real and tangible focus on diversity, partnering with universities, creating latticed career paths and multiple work formats, and leveraging the expertise of baby boomers, Generation X, and millennials to help mentor Generation Z workers into strong leaders.

How to Build a Multi-Generation Friendly Company Culture

To create a company culture in which each generation's needs are met begins with the CEO or business owner, as it must be a personal conviction of theirs to be successful. As leadership builds the culture, they also establish its mission, vision, and values.

These statements communicate the purpose and principles of the organization; how they are put into practice demonstrates what the company stands for. Statements alone are not enough. Everyone in the organization, from the CEO to the newly hired employee, must live them out every day. The perceptions of employees, customers, and vendors are determined by actions, not press releases.

In addition to setting the company culture, the CEO should be directly involved in the training of their managers. This position within the company has become an even more vital role, as managers are the conduit from leadership to the employees. They are responsible for leading their teams, communicating, and living out the company culture. The role of a manager is becoming more of a coach, leading and protecting their team members.

Providing regular, ongoing feedback regarding job performance is crucial, as it gives employees clear answers to the questions of "How am I doing?" and "Is my job safe?". Instead of dreading the annual review, employees will become more confident in their roles, and that allows them to bring their best effort and attitude to work every day.

To use an illustrative example, a couple of years ago, I received a call from an executive of a manufacturing company asking for some time to talk about their company culture. The initial issue they raised was that there was an atmosphere of tension in the company workspace; indeed, it was palpable as soon as they entered the facility.

This was having an impact on employee morale, turnover, personal and professional relationships, productivity, and the ability to deliver on customer expectations. The management team had been considering several options, including suspensions or terminations, changing of roles within the company, and scaling back the number of production lines.

As part of our due diligence process, we conduct discovery meetings with the executive team, members of mid-level management, and a select group of employees to get a comprehensive overview of what is really going on within a company at all levels. This is a critically important part of the process we use at White Water Consulting. Gaining insight and understanding from people with differing perspectives provides greater clarity and helps us understand the real issues that need to be addressed. Only dealing with what is seen at the surface does not resolve the deeper issues at the source.

During the discovery meetings, we learned that there were tensions between the multiple generations at the company, and in some cases, between those working together on the same teams. A couple of the millennial employees wanted to make some recommendations on how to improve the shipping process, which had been in place for almost twenty-five years without change. In fact, the technology and methodologies were also unchanged.

However, the shift and shipping managers dismissed the ideas before they could be heard.

Another incident occurred within the sales team, when one of the newer and younger sales reps began experiencing great success using different approaches to presenting and selling the products than the more senior reps were accustomed to. It probably did not help that the senior reps were not experiencing the same degree of success at the time, and they began to view and treat their younger co-workers with disrespect.

There was disharmony on the production, shipping, and sales teams, and there was a lack of desire by all parties involved to communicate. The animosity continued to grow between the younger generation and the more experienced managers who were primarily baby boomers.

Our first recommendation was to bring each of the teams together to air their differences in the hopes of closing the gaps through communication. After lengthy meetings, we determined that some progress had been made, but the parties were still at an impasse. The second recommendation was for the HR manager to put together an employee survey made up of questions pertaining to work, suggestions on how to make the culture better, and what each employee was passionate about doing outside of work.

The magic happened when areas of common personal interest outside of work were discovered. People realized that they shared interests in things such as sports, sports teams, hunting, physical activity, and virtual tastings. Relationships were formed, communication started, respect was established, and trust was built. The CEO said in a note of appreciation that for the first time in years, the company had a cohesive team that worked together to carry out the mission and vision of the company. Mission accomplished!

A crucial part of helping all generations feel that their needs are being met is making sure they have the chance to feel heard, seen, and valued. Give them opportunities to develop their skills and have a career path for the future. Open up options to choose what is best for them and for their current situation. Provide flexible benefit plans to choose from, such as offering ways for people to sell back part of their unused PTO to generate additional funds to then pay down student loans or buy long-term care insurance through the group benefit.

For those that want to continue to work into their retirement years, it is important to be a lifelong student, continuing to develop their skills and knowledge. For younger generations of workers, it is invaluable to have access to the wealth of knowledge that comes from experience. Pairing a baby boomer or a Gen Xer with a millennial or Gen Zer via a mentoring program adds exceptional value to the current team and will help develop future leadership.

Do not assume that this is a mentoring relationship in which only the older experienced person is serving as the mentor, as it is important to know that the younger employee can often add just as much value to their counterpart. Investing in your people is one of the greatest choices that any company can make, as it provides a great return on investment through higher employee engagement.

People, regardless of generation, want to believe that the work they are doing is meaningful and is having a positive impact in their community and on society. Leadership that wants to create a world-class culture, where people's needs are being met, must do everything they can to let their people know they are appreciated, are being heard, and are respected. Train and develop your people. Trust them. Empower them and then hold them accountable. People are every company's greatest asset!

If you want to find out how your company fares in terms of the generations working together, take our online assessment at <u>www.chuckcooper.info</u>.

Key Takeaways

- Recognize that every generation is different and have differing perspectives based on their life experiences.

- Having multi-generations in the workplace can mean more opportunities for success, but it can also lead to more challenges depending on how management handles the opportunity.

- To learn more about how to build trust with your multi-generational team, click here: https://whitewaterconsulting.net/building-trust-with-your-multigenerational-team/.

Unprecedented

Chapter 4: HR Best Practices

"The only waste of human resources is letting them go unused."
Mark Victor Hansen

Mark kept checking his emails, waiting for one in particular: the HR audit. It had been done a few weeks ago and they said it would be back today. Mark was nervous for the results. He had worked hard over the last two years to make the positive changes needed in his company, and felt he had done well. Now, it was time to see if what he had done was enough.

Finally, the email came through and Mark opened it quickly and smiled. With the exception of a few small areas, they had passed the HR audit with flying colors. He called together his management team and shared the good news with them. He also sent a congratulatory email to the entire company, thanking them for all their hard work in making this happen.

They were now ready for growth and Mark was excited. "Watch out world, here we come!"

What Are HR Best Practices?

I cannot say it often or emphatically enough: the greatest resource in any company, no matter how large or small, is its people. Having the right practices, procedures, and infrastructure to help support and develop their employees is crucial to every business. Companies depend on their people, and a properly functioning human resources department or outsource company is how they take care of them.

Effective company leadership works towards identifying ways to make their company stronger, and HR plays a vital role in talent acquisition and retention, creating the corporate culture, enhancing employee engagement, and communicating the company's values.

Best practices in human resources are management processes that have been proven to work universally, are based on examination of past results, and are aimed at improving infrastructure and results. Effective HR focuses on the needs of the organization and its people by striving to understand what motivates employees and enables them to bring the best version of themselves to work each day.

HR best practices help guide companies to select the right people to fill positions, give training and development to help their team grow, and provide the tools and skills needed to fulfill the vision of the organization.

As we discussed in the last chapter, the landscape of business and employment is always changing. With each new generation, the needs and challenges facing companies and their employees evolve—sometimes in very dramatic ways.

Even before the pandemic, social and employee focus had shifted strongly towards inclusion, diversity, growth, and contribution. Management hierarchies that center around uniformity, structure, and command and control will no longer be as effective. The pandemic has since brought a tsunami of changes and massive upheaval to how HR departments will need to function moving forward.

In a report by McKinsey & Company, they stated, "We shouldn't expect the old models to be a fit for purpose in today's environment as they are really mechanistic by design. They're built to solve for uniformity, bureaucracy, and control, which are goals that undercut what companies now prioritize such as creativity, speed, and accountability. The answer isn't to modify the old models, but to replace them with something radically better."

The new models replacing the previous power-based hierarchies are flat, agile, adaptable, collaborative, human-centric, and authentic. The focus is on leadership development, company culture, and the employee experience.

Benefits of Doing an HR Audit

We all instinctively flinch at the notion of an audit. Our minds fill with images of judgmental tax collectors scouring through our personal finances in search of money we might have to pay. Auditing processes and procedures as a form of proactive troubleshooting, however, are incredibly valuable.

An HR audit is, in part, used to determine any gaps in compliance between a company's policies and procedures and what is required by state and federal laws. At other levels, an HR audit helps owners and managers better understand the needs and priorities of their employees, as well as revealing how well the company vision has been communicated and is being fulfilled, or not.

HR audits compare a business's current practices to best practices of top-performing companies in order to help managers either strengthen current practices or pivot and adjust to changes within the workplace.

The report following an HR audit provides clarity about the realities of how well the business is functioning, as well as a list of actions that need to be taken to fill in the gaps with regards to compliance and to build, or maintain, a solid HR foundation within the organization.

When we go on-site to help companies perform an HR audit, it will typically take about a day to a day and a half to complete. Our approach adapts, depending on the size of the company and if they have employees in multiple states, for example. With most businesses, however, we typically find somewhere between twelve and twenty-four different items for them to work on. These include areas where they can improve compliance or incorporate best practices to help their company grow stronger.

We typically look at things such as what is included in the current employee handbook, and how long it has been since the handbook was updated. We examine job descriptions for each of the positions within the company and what policies are in place for topics ranging from discrimination to vacation and paid time off. We look at recruiting and onboarding processes, as well as all the onboarding forms that employees are required to complete. We also inspect employee benefits very closely.

As part of the process, we check the I-9 forms and related documentation they have, including where and how they are stored. If an official governmental audit ever takes place, it is vital that they can access everything they have requested; however, we strongly recommend that I-9s and supporting documentation be stored in a separate file. A recommended resource to help with I-9 compliance is the U.S. Citizenship and Immigration Services website: https://www.uscis.gov/.

One of the audits we helped with was for a manufacturing company. At the time, they had around 130 employees and, for the most part, had fairly good HR policies and procedures in place. Because they were so focused on trying to minimize the cost of payroll, one of the corners they cut was with their I-9 forms.

As a result, they wound up having approximately thirty employees without the proper documentation to work legally. In the U.S., employees are required to complete the I-9 and provide the required documentation within the first three days of employment.

Once such a situation is found, the employer must inform the employee that they do not have the appropriate documentation and are required to provide valid documentation immediately or they will be automatically terminated. In that particular case, of those thirty employees without proper documentation, only five were able to remedy it in time, and the rest had to be terminated.

It was sad. These were good people, working hard every day; they just did not have the proper documentation and the company had let those details and procedures fall through the cracks to minimize costs. As a result, the company lost twenty-five employees and those workers lost their livelihoods.

Many entrepreneurs tend to view HR as a must-have early in the business cycle. Once they feel the business is up on its feet, they forget about it and treat HR as a finished and set machine. Not only is this incorrect, but it leaves them blinded to what is going on, only able to deal with problems and messes after they have occurred. They become trapped in a purely reactive mode. Companies that proactively recognize that HR is a strategic part of their organization manage it with the same level of focus as sales and marketing.

The pandemic has dramatically changed the workplace environment by forcing companies to transition from physical workplaces to include remote work and hybrid work models. Such significant changes in the workplace require changes to current policies to ensure they protect the company by clearly communicating expectations and employment guidelines to the employees, as well as making sure company procedures remain in compliance.

As a result of all this change and upheaval, most small and mid-size companies are now conducting HR audits far more frequently, some of them for the first time in several years. As a standard practice, companies should conduct a full-scale HR audit every one to two years, with micro-audits conducted once every six months in order to allow for some course correction throughout the year.

Earlier in the book, we talked about a company that had great success at launch, but over time wound up imploding because they did not have the HR infrastructure needed to support their growth. That implosion could have been prevented if the company's leadership approach had included implementing HR best practices as part of their initial launch, rather than simply focusing on financial gain. There is an investment when you manage proactively, but the cost is much greater when you operate reactively.

HR audits continue to be valuable throughout the life cycle of a business. Companies with strong HR infrastructure and company culture enjoy longer employee tenure, higher employee engagement, and provide a higher multiple, making the company more valuable and appealing to future investment and potential acquisition.

How HR Saves Money, Time, and Resources for Small to Mid- Size Businesses

Within the first three years after launching their company, entrepreneurs often consider HR to be a financial drain, since it does not generate any direct or immediate revenue. This is why many small and mid-size business owners operate with a reactive mindset and will often simply delegate everything HR-related to the person handling the finances.

It is an understandable impulse, as payroll, payroll taxes, insurance, and HR compliance all pull cash away from the pocket of the owner. Controllers or accountants are typically focused on minimizing and managing expenditures, which can be both positive and negative in a start-up organization, depending on where their efforts are targeted.

As someone who has worked with many small and mid-size companies, I often found myself sitting in the finance office trying to find a solution that would benefit the company while fitting within a small budget.

If the company had a business plan that included a focus on future growth and training and development of their people, it was easier to shift the perceptions of HR to one of investment rather than an expense.

The bottom line is that no matter how large or small the business, it relies on its people. If the employees of the company are not being managed effectively, and if they are not being kept informed, supported, motivated, and listened to, then their productivity drops. When productivity drops, so too do the success and profits of the business.

Deciding Whether to Build an HR Team or Outsource

As an entrepreneur, you have accepted the risk of walking away from the security of a paycheck and employee benefits package, and have invested a large amount of your time, finances, and relationships into starting your business. You are passionate about the vision you have and how your product or service is going to fill an important need in the marketplace. It is because of this passion that entrepreneurs are often the leaders in sales and service delivery.

Businesses, however, are only as strong as their leadership's ability to focus on the steps necessary for them to make business ideas succeed. A key component in a business plan needs to be the role that HR is going to play in the organizational start-up, as this sets the tone for how company leadership is going to view their people. Are they going to see them as assets or liabilities? I shall say it again: people are every company's greatest asset.

I am a firm believer in HR outsourcing, as it allows you to remain focused on growing and managing your business while partnering with a company that brings HR expertise. They become a strategic partner, working on your behalf to provide services such as HR compliance, payroll, work comp, employee benefits, and benefits administration, as well as other occasional strategic HR services needed over the life cycle of the business.

In the early years of a business, entrepreneurs often do not have the resources or experience to properly handle HR oversight, and all too frequently are tempted to think of their business as too small to worry about it. For many business owners, there is also a point where the volume of work outpaces their ability to manage everything effectively and efficiently.

Regardless of how old or new or large or small, every business needs to have someone overseeing and managing their human resources. As an entrepreneur, you must keep your expertise, passion, and vision focused on the essentials of your business. Outsourcing those areas that are necessary but outside of your area of expertise ultimately saves you time, money, and protects the longevity of your business.

The overall cost of outsourcing, as opposed to building an internal HR team, is the equivalent of hiring a group of subject matter experts at a fraction of the cost. The clients that have followed our recommendations and utilized the services of an HR outsourcing company effectively have always wound up with a solid HR infrastructure built within eighteen to thirty-six months. After that, we advise conducting another HR audit to determine whether it is best to continue outsourcing or if it is time to bring things in-house and begin building an internal HR team.

We worked with a client who had seven employees at start-up and followed our guidance on selecting an HR outsourcing company to handle the people side of the business while they focused on growing revenue and controlling expenses for the first five years of operation.

After the company had grown to approximately 150 employees with offices located throughout the country and had begun to add people at the corporate office to handle recruiting and onboarding, we recommended conducting a fresh HR audit. The audit revealed that it would be in their best interest to develop a plan for transitioning HR in-house, ideally within the following twelve months.

The client was able to make the transition while continuing to grow successfully before ultimately being acquired. Key factors in making the transition were having a strong HR foundation in place and effectively using the HR company and its services.

Simply hiring employees is not enough to make your business successful or sustainable, and profit-focused, control-based management models are no longer a workable fit for the current nature and priorities of the workforce. The quality of your HR policies, practices, and procedures can make or break your company because—say it with me now—every company's greatest asset is its people.

Key Takeaways

- HR audits help owners and managers better understand the needs and priorities of their people.

- Using a platform like Mineral (a.k.a., ThinkHR) will be beneficial, as it can continuously monitor state and federal employment law changes.

- With the tsunami of changes occurring due to COVID-19, how will your HR need to evolve to support the priorities of creativity, speed, and accountability?

- It is important to recognize that being proactive when it comes to HR requires an investment of time and finances upfront; however, the cost of being reactive is considerably greater.

Chapter 5: How to Outsource

"Do what you do best, outsource the rest."
Peter Drucker

When we reach the end of our lives, we tend to reflect back over our time here on earth. Our greatest regrets are often those things we chose not to do because of fear, uncertainty, and doubt. On the flip side, our greatest joys come from taking calculated risks and the fulfilling moments born from pushing past our fears and beyond our comfort zones.

Many people have great ideas and dream of starting their own business. A large percentage of them, however, let the fear and uncertainty of risk stop them from taking even the first steps toward launching their company. One of the main reasons for this book is to encourage more entrepreneurs to take the risk and launch their company while arming them with tools that will help them be successful. The courage to try is what entrepreneurship is all about!

When you begin your own business, you must manage all the different aspects of the operation yourself, including sales, marketing, service, and finance. As the operation grows, you will reach a point where you can no longer do everything. You cannot continue to work twenty-four hours a day, seven days a week for the rest of your life. You will have to hire your first employee.

Once you make that hire, you have started a second business of being an employer. You are now responsible for leadership, guidance, payroll, payroll taxes, workers comp, and providing employee benefits. This is where an important decision has to be made by the owner or the leadership team.

Many entrepreneurs make the mistake of trying to handle the entire role of being an employer on their own. They try to manage the HR for their company themselves when they have limited to no experience doing so, and wind up creating increased liability for their company due to a lack of knowledge and understanding. By trying to handle all of the employment-related matters on top of all the other business operations, they increase the risk of mistakes being made and things being missed.

Even though they are trying to minimize expenses, mistakes in HR, such as payroll, taxes, or the proper filing of documentation, can be extremely costly. We all have our limits and no one is good at everything. It is important to remember where your strengths and skills are, and what fuels your passions and excitement, so you can delegate the other areas to those better suited or with more expertise.

This is why we try and help our clients visualize splitting their company into two parts. The first is management of operations. The second encompasses the people-related tasks, such as payroll, taxes, benefits, state and federal compliance, and risk mitigation. Both are equally important, requiring focus and expertise. As the owner, you need to remain focused on the first part of the business and allow a strategic partner to handle the second.

It is vitally important for the entrepreneur and their leadership team to stay concentrated on their areas of core competence. You need to pick a lane and stay in it, remaining focused. So often I see entrepreneurs (and I've been guilty of this myself) who start out focused, but then something new comes along. The thought, "Oh, yeah, I can make an investment and add this into what I am currently doing," seems innocent enough at first.

Before long, however, our plates start to overflow. Our focus, time, and energy become spread too thin. Our stress and exhaustion increase, and we start making mistakes. We begin to miss things that, in turn, further increase our stress and exhaustion. In the end, the interesting new thing winds up taking away rather than adding to our businesses.

For those areas outside of our expertise, rather than simply trying to hire people to fill the gaps, in the early growing years of the business it is best to look at outsourcing. Whether it is HR, marketing, or even sales, it is important to try and be as efficient with the dollars spent, to be as good a steward over your resources, as possible. Outsourcing can be an excellent way to place your areas of weakness or inexperience into the hands of those with the appropriate expertise.

When Is It Time to Start Using HR Practices in Your Business?

Based on my twenty-five years of experience, the moment to begin using proper HR practices is when you hire your first employee. Even before that moment, you need to map how you are going to handle HR as part of your initial business plan. Look at HR from a strategic standpoint and be proactive. That way, you have clarity about how you are going to approach HR before you start to need it—indeed, before you have even launched the company.

An employee handbook is one of the first documents an employer needs, as it is a valuable communication resource for both the employer and the employees. The handbook contains the company history, mission, vision, values, policies, procedures, and employee benefits. It sets clear expectations for the employees, while also defining employee rights and stating your legal obligations as an employer.

When there is an employee issue, such as harassment, discrimination, or other employee-related discrepancy, the handbook is the first point of reference. This makes it crucially important that all businesses have one that is updated regularly to create transparency and consistency throughout the organization.

We typically see that companies wait until they reach the 5–10 employee range before they begin to develop a more formal HR infrastructure. That, however, is like waiting until your house is on fire to buy a fire extinguisher or to get insurance. There is an enormous number of factors that can impact the needs of your company with regards to HR, and it is far better to be as prepared as possible for them in advance.

The state your company is in can affect the form and pacing of your HR requirements. What are the growth projections for the next twelve to twenty-four months? When will you need to hire more employees, and how many? Remember, the needs of a company with five employees are different from one with ten, twenty, or fifty people.

As an entrepreneur, you need to have your plans ready in advance, and to have your infrastructure in place beforehand. That way, you can simply move on to the next step when the time comes. Leaving things undone or incomplete until you need them leaves you in a purely reactive mode, constantly on your heels and in danger of getting swamped. Establish your HR plans before you launch, which may mean being prepared to outsource your HR services the moment you hire your first employee.

The Two Main Types of HR Outsourcing: PEO and ASO

HR outsourcing companies fall into two main categories: PEO or Professional Employer Organizations, and ASO or Administrative Services Organizations. Both have their strengths and weaknesses, and one might be a better fit for you and your business. To help clarify their differences, we will look at them in terms of six key areas of HR.

Employee–Employer Relationship

A key distinction between a PEO and an ASO is the concept of co-employment. In a co-employment scenario, the outside entity becomes sort of an honorary member of your management team; they are an active strategic partner with partial authority over and on behalf of your employees. In a simple service outsourcing arrangement, certain tasks and procedures are delegated to an outside entity; they crunch the numbers, do the paperwork, and send it back to you.

A PEO operates as a co-employer. This is beneficial when it comes to negotiating health insurance and other compensatory elements because a PEO is seen as representing all of the employees from all of the companies they work with. This means they could have the weight of tens of thousands of employees behind them, thus giving them much greater purchasing and negotiating power than you would as a small business owner.

Business owners often hesitate or dismiss the value of PEOs because they are afraid of losing control of their employees. The perception is that the employees will no longer work for them, and the PEO will become the employer of record. To be clear, the client can maintain control and direction over their employees within the PEO relationship. You are their client. The PEO works for you.

An ASO only assists in an advisory capacity, and takes on your administrative tasks rather than you having to hire more full-time staff to handle them. The only relationship an ASO has with your employees is like that of any HR department. They administer employee relations compliance, and can help with the development of employee handbooks, policies, and procedures. Ultimately, though, hiring, firing, and enforcement remains with you.

Health Insurance

Because the PEOs have tens of thousands of employees on their books, they can offer extremely affordable health and dental insurance plans. They can also provide other types of employee benefits such as 401(k), life, disability, and other voluntary benefits that you would find in much larger organizations. The PEO handles all negotiations and administration. Some organizations even leverage the insurance benefits offered by their PEO as a recruiting tool.

An ASO can help you find the right kind of insurance for your organization and even help you negotiate your rates and coverage. They can also help you administer the program for your employees. The only limits to your health and dental benefits are what you can afford, as pricing is based on your group's data. It is much easier to have an ASO help you find the right kind of coverage than it is trying to navigate the marketplace on your own.

State Unemployment Insurance

A PEO takes care of all of this. It handles the unemployment insurance deductions and payments and, because it has a huge pool of employees, its risk of claims is reduced. Additionally, the larger PEOs provide free job performance improvement and training resources, which their clients can offer to employees who may want to take on a new challenge or pursue a new direction with their employer. This helps to keep employees engaged, and can cut down on the potential need to terminate employment.

With an ASO, the unemployment insurance rate is solely based on the number of claims generated by your business, which is great if you only have a few claims. A PEO could generate significantly more claims by the sheer size of the organization. However, ASOs (just like a PEO) also have resources available to assist with hiring and retention, which should help limit the exposure to unemployment claims.

Workers' Compensation

A PEO can act as a shield for its partner, depending on the contract. It takes on the bulk or all of the responsibility that comes with offering workers' compensation insurance, such as liability for insurance claims, safety, and loss. They can do this because their risk is spread over a much larger pool of employees.

As a result, small to mid-sized businesses can wind up paying rates usually reserved for larger employers, since they are paying for this coverage through their contract with the PEO. Just as with workers' compensation, though, the PEO will help its client look for areas where it can most effectively mitigate risk.

With an ASO, the coverage is the responsibility of the employer. An ASO can help a business find the right kind of coverage and negotiate a policy. The ASO can also manage the administration of that policy, and handle any claims on behalf of the business. ASOs will work with a client company to suggest ways to mitigate risk should the business's employees be prone to physical injury, like in a warehouse or construction business.

Since there is no large pool to help spread the risk, however, all the responsibility and liability for any insurance claims, safety, and loss rest solely with the client company—your company. Should there be a claim, the ASO can help from an administrative standpoint, but that is all.

Payroll

A PEO will take care of your payroll functions, but it will pay federal payroll taxes under its federal employer identification number because your employees are being handled as its employees. The PEO collects all the federal withholding, Social Security, and Medicare. As far as the IRS is concerned, in this scenario, you technically have no employees.

An ASO will handle all of your payroll functions, but it will all be done under your company's federal employee identification number. With regards to the IRS, they remain as your employees with all the commensurate duties and responsibilities.

Cost

The fees of PEOs are typically higher; however, the net difference in cost may be less than an ASO combined with the company's current internal costs. A full, in-depth process and cost analysis conducted by a Subject Matter Expert (SME) is strongly recommended, as it can be challenging to fully understand a PEO's proposal and how their fees may affect your business costs overall.

There is an incredibly wide range of prices that vary from a percentage of payroll to a fixed cost per employee per month. A full-service PEO will charge upwards of $100–$250 per employee per month, but it will come with a high level of service, resources, online options for employees to sign up for benefits, training, videos, and assessments. As with most things, you get what you pay for.

ASOs typically charge a flat rate, which is usually lower per employee per month than a PEO. Each service you need can be purchased à la carte, whether you need help with compliance issues, taxes, or workers' compensation insurance. You pay only for what you need.

It is important to clearly identify the requirements of your company so you can determine which of the services and resources you will need. That way, you can choose the type of outsourcing that best fits your situation.

Too many times, we have seen business owners make the decision to move forward with a PEO, then reach the end of the year and realize the only services they utilized were payroll, work comp, and benefits. If you are comfortable with a co-employment relationship and having someone else carry the risk, then you will likely want to look at a PEO. If you just need a bit of help with administrative processes, an ASO may be your preference.

The key elements to remember are that we all have our strengths and priorities, none of us can do everything all the time, and it is far better to be ready in advance than scrambling after the fact.

The best recipe for success is to identify your strengths, where your time and efforts are best spent, and then build a plan that will let you stay in your ideal lane.

Delegating the tasks and areas that are outside our expertise can sometimes mean hiring employees or outsourcing to other entities. For most entrepreneurs, HR is a new and unfamiliar territory, especially in the early years of growing a new business. Having a plan in place to outsource HR concerns and tasks before you launch your business can be both a lifesaver and a key component for the success, growth, and potential longevity of your company.

If you are not sure what your company needs, I am here to help. Email me at chuck@whitewaterconsulting.net and let's book a time to talk. I can help you determine your company needs and the best resources to accomplish your goals.

Key Takeaways

- As the owner of the business, stay focused on the growth of the revenues, managing expenses, and mitigating liability, and allow a strategic partner with expertise to handle HR.

- Consider how you are going to handle HR, and include it in your business plan before you launch the company.

- Make sure you fully understand the differences between a PEO and an ASO model if you are going to outsource.

- When you decide to outsource HR, it is imperative that you use the HR services included regularly in order to obtain the greatest return on your investment.

Chapter 6: The Compliance Issue

"A compliance plan shows you have a system of checks in place."

Bruce Blehart

Katherine could not believe this was happening. There was a good chance that the government was going to close down her company, and possibly for good. How could accounting let this happen? They knew that it was part of their job to check.

The day before, the government had come in for a surprise audit and found that the security clearance required to work on their sensitive projects had not been kept up. Suddenly, twenty people were not able to work until they were cleared. Worse than that, she was told that because of this, they would either close her down or not give her company any more contracts. Either way spelled the death of her business, as it was 90 percent government-funded.

She talked to the head of accounting, who made a lame excuse about telling her a year ago that they needed an HR department to handle these things. She was not happy but saw that he was right. He had, in fact, told her the truth, and she ignored it because she did not want to "waste" precious money on something that did not produce an immediate ROI. Now, she wished she had.

Her only hope now was to beg for mercy from the government and hope that they give her a second chance to make it right.

Compliance is not sexy or a fun thing to talk about. Most people, including entrepreneurs, do not appreciate how many different regulations small and mid-size companies are required to comply with until they are in the role of being an employer. Then, they have their "Aha" moment. Understanding, addressing, and being prepared for these kinds of regulations are essential to the long-term success of a business.

By definition, compliance means "Conforming to a rule, such as a specification, policy, standard, or law" (Source: *Wikipedia*).

Within the corporate world, it is defined as the process of making sure your company and employees follow all laws, regulations, standards, and ethical practices that apply to the organization.

Many factors can impact which specific areas of compliance apply most prominently to a company, such as the particular industry, state, and the number of employees a company has. In general, however, most companies must comply with guidelines in the following areas:

1. **Tax Code** – Income tax, Estimated tax, Employment tax, Excise tax, Sales tax.

2. **Employment and Labor Laws** – OSHA, Wages and hours, Workplace safety, EEOC, ERISA, Family, and Medical Leave Act, and Posters.

3. **Antitrust Laws** – Sherman Act, Clayton Act, FTCA.

4. **Advertising** – Dodd-Frank, UDAAP, TCPA.

5. **Environmental Regulations** – EPA, CFR titles 10, 18, 21, use of EDMS.

6. **Email Marketing** – UDAAP, FTCA.

7. **Privacy** – HIPAA, FCRA, ECPA.

8. **Licensing and Permits** – Local, State, Federal, Zoning, Fire, CPS, EAR.

9. **Insurance** – Medical, Liability, Safety.

10. **Reporting Payroll data** – FUTA, FICA, W-2.

11. **Sales Tax** – Local, State, Federal, Nexus.

Compliance is mandatory for all companies, including small and medium-sized ones. As a result, entrepreneurs and managers need to know how to implement individual measures based on current procedures and standards.

Business owners often cite lack of time and financial resources as reasons why they are not in compliance; however, it is typically due to a lack of concern.

Though any aspect of a business can have compliance-related concerns, from a strategic standpoint, they can be divided into two initial categories: external compliance and internal compliance. External compliance deals with all the ways that a company impacts the outside world environmentally, financially, and socially. Internal compliance deals with all the impacts that occur between the members of the company, between the owners and employees, and between the employees themselves.

External Compliance

There is any number of local, state, and federal agencies that regulate and oversee how businesses conduct themselves when it comes to environmental impacts, financial practices, and social engagement. A crucial step to forming and eventually implementing any plan for how to ensure your company is properly in compliance is to first identify and understand which agencies and regulations are going to apply.

Simply identifying them is not enough. Business owners need to have a full understanding of how their company is going to operate and what adjustments they might have to make to their plans and designs in order to ensure they are in compliance with all the relevant regulations.

The approach needs to be proactive and long-term forward-thinking. Fines and fees for violating regulations can be fatally expensive and waiting until a mess has already occurred will mean it is too late to do anything to prevent it. Problems can occur because things get mismanaged and fall through the cracks. All too often, however, compliance problems are generated out of an attempt to cut corners.

Several years ago, I was speaking with the owner of a small business who had founded his manufacturing company almost thirty years prior. The business had approximately twenty-five employees, and the owner had created a very comfortable lifestyle for himself. During my conversations with him, I quickly realized he acted as the alpha and the omega in the company chain of command. He was the sum total of the decision-making process, and his employees knew it, as many of them had invested their entire careers working for the company.

The manufacturing business was located very close to a large body of water that was monitored by the State Department of Natural Resources as well as the Environmental Protection Agency. Over time, new laws and regulations regarding liquid containment and stormwater runoff had been passed, but as there had been little to no enforcement, the business owner chose to disregard the new legislation.

He decided not to spend the money and resources necessary to implement the operational updates. Nor did he put in place, or even develop, any plans for doing so in the future. No one was actively forcing him, so why spend money he did not have to? This is a classic example of a reactive rather than a proactive mindset.

One summer day in July, however, a major storm came through, bringing several inches of rain and high winds, which damaged the buildings and flooded the manufacturing facility. Due to the facility not having the necessary, updated containment structures around the storage tanks, stormwater contaminated with manufacturing waste flooded the surrounding area, thus polluting the nearby river and destroying wildlife.

Although the event was caused by natural forces, the owner was forced to pay monetary damages for the non-compliance with the stormwater discharge and a one-time penalty for wildlife damage. He was required to develop a plan to provide temporary containment and to bring the facility into proper compliance before operations could restart, with an additional daily fine for each day the business was not in compliance. The owner elected to shut the business down rather than spend the money needed to comply.

On multiple occasions, I have seen a company board and leadership elect to close or sell the business rather than spend the time and resources to upgrade their facilities and processes. For years, compliance has been perceived solely through the lens of finance and, thus, shuffled aside or ignored in attempts to cut costs. However, today, as companies focus on the inclusion of stakeholders, leadership is tasked with making decisions more focused on the environmental, social, and governance impacts.

This shift has forced many companies to become much more deliberate in their operational decision-making philosophy and to extend the amount of time they allow and assign to the decision-making process when it comes to procedural planning and compliance.

Internal Compliance

Even though there are many regulations governing how businesses as entities interact with the world around them, there are also long lists of agencies and regulations with regards to how companies impact their employees and how those employees impact one another.

On the company-to-employee side, once an entrepreneur grows into taking on staff and becoming an employer, there are a host of local, state, and federal regulations to be aware of and comply with, such as payroll, income tax, workplace safety, hiring and firing practices, and medical benefits.

Obviously, HR is the funnel through which many of these processes will be implemented, monitored and where any issues or problems will first be reported. In the last chapter, we talked about several of the most common aspects of the business that HR, either internal to the company or outsourced, handles most often. In the next chapter, we are going to talk about one of the largest subject areas in the HR territory: dealing with the ISMs of discrimination. When it comes to looking after the well-being of the company's employees, though, it is more of a universal operational issue rather than strictly an HR concern.

Everyone from the top executives to the frontline workers needs to be aware of policies and procedures, be informed about the necessary and relevant regulations, and participate in making sure all protocols are being followed. Compliance procedures are not of much use if no one knows about them or is not following through on them. The more communication and engagement at all levels, the better.

Now, post-pandemic, rather than having silos within the leadership for finance and for, operations and HR, the walls are coming down. All departments and levels should have visibility across the organization. If a company is truly going to view its people as their greatest asset, then why shouldn't HR be viewed as a vital part of the management team?

HR is now becoming involved in things that are happening on the finance and legal side, management is having more direct contact with workers, and frontline employees have a more open and direct voice in the decisions and actions of the company.

The focus is shifting away from segmented hierarchies toward more collaborative-style models. This not only generates greater levels of engagement and belonging, which then increase productivity, but it also keeps conversations and awareness around procedures and compliance active instead of passive.

Regulations are changing and constantly updating on both the internal and external sides, so simply forming a start-up plan is not enough. Compliance is a garden that needs constant tending, and the more hands actively involved, the easier it becomes, and the less likely mistakes will get made.

Effective Approaches and Best Practices

Being in compliance requires companies to take a proactive approach and focus on concern for their people, including operating processes and employee safety. The policies, procedures, and employment practices that small and medium-size companies develop are directly influenced by the business's ownership and leadership.

We always recommend that business owners look at soliciting the assistance of an experienced professional third party, such as an outside HR consultant, PEO, or ASO, to help them create their policies, procedures, and even their employee handbook. It is crucial that leadership invest the time and resources to have strong policies and procedures in place so they can mitigate future risks that could be fatal for a young company.

Conducting a compliance risk analysis of your business can help raise awareness among leadership and employees and is something that should be done on a recurring basis. Just because there were no weeds in the garden last time it was checked does not mean there might not be some poking through now.

Let your employees be a part of the process. Get them involved on committees and within the community so they are spending time working together and away from the workplace. Creating personal relationships builds community. As a business owner, I want all my people to be a part of an environment that allows them to be at their best every day.

I want them to leave at the end of the day knowing the work they did was for a purpose bigger than themselves. A person's self-worth is greatly impacted by the experiences they have and the relationships they build over time. Focus on building your company culture by keeping the core values front and center, developing curriculums to make training consistent throughout the organization, maintaining regular communications, and providing examples of how employees can live out those core values.

The final recommendation in this section is for companies to purchase an Employer Practices Liability Insurance (EPLI) policy. This coverage will help protect the company if litigation is filed by a current or past employee based on management actions. This policy will have a deductible paid by the insured and will provide funds that can be used to settle claims.

Research non-profit Just Capital has been doing a study called "The Just 100". It is an annual listing of the top 100 companies in the U.S. that are doing things in accordance with the current general priorities of American society. They are paying a fair wage, caring for their employees, and giving more to charity and to community organizations than the average publicly traded company. They are also generating earnings of 4.5 percent to 5 percent more than companies that are not.

They are paying out more in dividends simply because the practices they have are in alignment with what the American people feel are the right things to do. This is something that is really starting to pick up a lot of traction in the last couple of years.

As we look to the future of work, the criteria that socially conscious investors are using to assess and screen companies—environmental, social, and governance—will not only be something we are hearing a lot more about but are likely to become the dominant model in the business landscape.

Key Takeaways

- An entrepreneur's commitment to compliance speaks to the character of leadership, which will impact the company's culture and the relationship with its stakeholders.

- As leadership continues to evolve, the breaking down of departmental silos within the company will allow management to make decisions with a holistic perspective.

- Identify ways for employees to serve together on committees and to be seen as having a positive impact within the community where the business operates.

- Check with your insurance broker regarding your options for EPLI coverage.

- To learn more about the Just 100 companies, go to: https://www.cnbc.com/2022/01/11/the-just-100-list.html.

Unprecedented

Chapter 7: How to Deal With the ISMs

"The inability to rise above one's inherited ism and ideology
makes one live and die a fool, just a folly."
Fakeer Ishavardas

We all have biases in the ways we look at the world. The experiences we have had shape how we perceive things. We are naturally inclined to prefer the things we know, recognize, and are familiar with. If something is unfamiliar or unknown, there is a chance it could be dangerous, and our survival instincts tell us to fear it just in case.

Our biases are this instinct at work. They are reflexive attempts to understand the world and steer us away from potential dangers. Biases fall into two main categories: explicit and implicit. Our explicit biases are the ones we are aware of. We notice them, and we can control them if we choose to.

Our implicit biases are the ones we are not conscious of; they happen instinctively and can heavily influence our lives without us ever really being aware of them. We can root them out and become aware of them, but it takes work and, most often, some outside help.

Biases are not automatically dangerous or harmful. They are born from our survival instincts, but if we are not aware of them, they can wind up making our decisions for us or distorting the way we view the world around us to the point of changing our choices as well.

Speaking with hundreds of businesses over the last twenty years, I have seen these biases at play in the workplace. For example, within HR, our biases can tilt the wording we use in job postings, skewing the tone of the requirements in discriminatory ways with regard to education or ethnic background.

As with all things, the more we know about our biases, the better we understand them and the better armed we are to confront and deal with them. There are many kinds of common biases we all engage in that are fairly easy to recognize.

Authority bias is an inclination to view those in a position of authority as being of greater trustworthiness and character. Affinity bias is looking more favorably on those who share our worldview. Conformity bias means preferring choices that go with the flow and enable us to feel a sense of belonging. Horn (or halo) bias is where a single experience in a particular instance—either good or bad—then defines how we will view any future experience of it. Confirmation bias is seeking and believing only information that agrees with our existing ideas and opinions.

If we let our biases go unchecked, they can grow more powerful and take control of our thoughts and actions. They can become ISMs and lead to outright discrimination. It is important to understand that all people have internal biases, but as entrepreneurs and business owners, it is imperative that we do everything we can to prevent discrimination in any form and at every level of our organization.

As mandated by state and federal law, companies cannot discriminate against or harass applicants, employees, or customers on the basis of race, color, religion, sex, national origin, age, disability, or genetic information. For business owners, avoiding discrimination is not simply a concern of treating people nicely; it is a legal requirement that can result in serious penalties if violated.

The laws in this area have been increasing, expanding, and growing more detailed over the past several decades, but issues around discrimination have really started to play out in the last three to five years. Part of it has to do with the fact that, as a society, we are stepping up, speaking out, and saying "No" to things that we know are wrong.

For a long time, the status quo was one of management and ownership not only tolerating ISMs but also perpetuating or even encouraging them. While the laws aimed at preventing these kinds of discrimination have been getting stronger, it is in the past few years that social attitudes and activism have really powered up and started to truly change the landscape.

The three biggest ISMs that we tangle within small to mid-size businesses are racism, ageism, and sexism. These are issues and biases that have been around for many years and, sadly, are still prevalent today. The attitudes beneath them are deeply ingrained and tough to dislodge.

Racism

The current Merriam–Webster definition of racism describes it as "A belief that race is the primary determinant of human traits and capacities and that racial differences produce an inherent superiority of a particular race."

As we explore employment and discrimination in the workplace for the past two decades, there were more than 1.88 million complaints filed with the Equal Employment Opportunity Commission (EEOC). Despite state and federal laws addressing discrimination based on race, studies show that hiring bias against Black and Hispanic employees has not improved in more than twenty years. Latinos have seen only a modest drop in discrimination against them.

Race has had and continues to have a significant impact on one's chance of receiving consideration for a job opening. This leads to fewer callbacks, which lowers the chance of finding a job; it also leads to lower compensation offers and less leverage in negotiations because there are fewer options.

Regarding religious discrimination and work situations, the law forbids discrimination when it comes to any aspect of employment, including hiring, firing, pay, job assignments, promotions, payoff, training, fringe benefits, and any other term or condition of employment. Other forms of religious discrimination include clothing requirements that violate religious practices and prohibiting time for religious observance.

Harassment can include offensive remarks about a person's religious beliefs or practices. The harasser can be the victim's supervisor, a supervisor in another area, a co-worker, or someone who is not an employee of the employer, such as a client or a customer.

There are some practices that entrepreneurs can implement that will help eradicate racism in the workplace, including the following:

1. Post racism discrimination notices that describe what discrimination is and stress that it will not be tolerated.

2. Give workers the training they need so that they are aware of what makes their behavior illegal. Training should include providing information on the law as well as on company policy surrounding the issue.

3. Take on a no-tolerance policy. Employees need to understand that your company is simply not going to be lax when it comes to addressing issues surrounding discrimination.

4. Define a clear complaint process.

5. Specifically, address discrimination in employment policy.

Since 2020, racism has had a spotlight placed on it, particularly with regard to police misconduct, generating protests and riots in many of the country's largest cities. With the heightened emotions surrounding racism, there is a true need for calm, open communication, active listening, and empathy rather than being judgemental and allowing politics, social media, and news media to divide us.

As we talked about earlier, with affinity bias, we gravitate toward people like ourselves in appearance, beliefs, and background. Thus, it is our impulse to hire people who look like us, think like us, and share our beliefs. This leads to those we see as being different not being considered, hired, or promoted within the company.

One of the most common bias-generated barriers that employers can put up, perhaps without even realizing it, is around expected educational requirements for applicants. The tragic fact is that, on average, African Americans do not have the same level of opportunities for education as whites, Asians, or Hispanics.

In 2022, this topic has now become extremely politicized. We have let politics hijack the conversations around racism to a point where now, in the U.S., you are either in our camp or you are the enemy; it's the "us versus them" mentality. There is no common ground, and no conversations or dialogue are taking place.

As business owners, we must recognize there are differences between people and their experiences of life, that there have been issues in the past with regards to how those differences have been treated, and that those issues persist today. We have to focus our attention and our efforts on what is best for our company and our communities in the long term.

Ageism

Ageism is the discrimination against individuals or groups on the basis of their age. Ageism can take many forms, including prejudicial attitudes, discriminatory practices, or institutional policies and procedures that perpetuate stereotypical beliefs about age. In some cases, employees who experience ageism are left out of meetings, get talked over, or have their comments overlooked.

Over the years, there has been a perception that as one crosses into their mid-40s, and every five years going forward, management will be looking to remove that person from their position and replace them with a younger, less costly individual. This is a classic case of viewing your people as a line item on the company's financial statement and not as an asset.

According to a study done by AARP (formerly the American Association of Retired Persons) in 2020, 78 percent of older workers saw or experienced age discrimination in the workplace versus 61 percent in 2018.

In the same year, 76 percent of older workers saw age discrimination as a hurdle to finding a new job. Another report found that more than 50 percent of these older workers are prematurely pushed out of longtime jobs, and 90 percent of them never earn as much again.

Ageism in the workplace takes many forms; however, the three main areas are:

1. Recruitment and hiring, when younger applicants are shown favor simply because of their age.

2. On-the-job bias is when older workers receive fewer training opportunities, promotions, and rewards or are harassed.

3. Termination is when a company "freshens" its workforce or trims its budget by targeting senior employees for layoffs or encouraging them to retire.

Within larger companies, employees are viewed as "human capital," and they are seen as capital equipment. You buy it, assume it has a certain shelf life, and then you get rid of it and replace it with a new model.

We often think of ageism as only applying to people as they become older. Although that certainly occurs, it is important to recognize that it also happens to those younger in age as well. Any view that pre-qualifies or pre-disqualifies someone purely on the grounds of their age perpetuates ageism, and it is the responsibility of employers to ensure such practices are not being used in their companies.

Sexism

The definition of sexism is prejudice or discrimination based on sex. In most cases, the discrimination negatively targets women or individuals with differing gender identity. A major feature of sexism in the workplace is the stereotype that women are not as productive as men, they are moody, and that starting or raising a family renders them unreliable and less effective.

As we look back over the last twenty to thirty years, it is clear that women have been overlooked during the interview process, passed over for future promotions they are qualified for, and offered less pay than their male counterparts holding the same title and doing the same work. Those holding a large percentage of middle and upper-level management positions have been, and still are, older white males who are keeping their positions of power and control longer than ever before.

Women were unable to speak up about inequalities or discrimination because all the power dynamics were tilted against them. They were at the mercy of those in power who regarded them as lesser and would be risking their livelihoods and reputations by speaking out.

However, there is some good news. Through DE&I (diversity, equity, and inclusion) programs, there are more women being included on corporate boards and upper-level management positions. Even with the younger generations, the pay gap is narrowing. It is incumbent on a company's stakeholders to hold management accountable. Management must take actions that will generate genuine substance from DE&I programs and not just engage in appealingly worded marketing ploys that do nothing concrete to address the real issues.

Creating a Company Culture That Combats ISMs

A company's culture is set by its leader. There has to be an intense focus placed on the actions that support your culture, meaning that leadership has to fully engage. It needs to be a personal mission of the leader to not allow ISMs to be present in the company policies and procedures.

In companies that I have been a part of or companies that I have worked with, there were often instances of tension between leadership and HR. Comments were made, or actions were taken by leadership that went against company policy or procedure without any consequences, thus generating the view that company policies did not apply to everyone equally.

This was wrong then, and it is wrong today. It might have been very typical behavior in the past, but as society has evolved, leadership is now being held to a higher standard. In some cases, leaders are even being held accountable for incidents that happened decades earlier.

When you look at the ESG parts of governance, there are multiple studies illustrating that employees expect their leadership to take positions on political issues, either as a business owner or as the C -Suite. They want their leaders to speak out and want to work for a leader whose views and beliefs are in alignment with their own. We will continue to see people resign either because of a lack of such alignment or a failure of leadership to speak out.

It is crucial that the workplace environment of your company makes your people feel safe and secure. Establish open communication and schedule sessions to raise awareness and minimize discriminatory behaviors at work. Be empathetic, transparent, and authentic. Enable them to provide examples of when they have seen or experienced ISMs and share how it made them feel.

Have employees and leaders discuss how the issues they experienced were dealt with or not, and make it safe to offer ideas and suggestions for how to prevent them or deal with them in the future. Your employees will want to know how you view these issues and what actions you had taken when you encountered bad behavior or had it reported to you.

Ensure you are giving them the message that the organization is going to treat everyone fairly regardless of age, gender, sex, or race. Part of doing that is open and authentic communication. The other part starts with the values of the organization and having the right policies and procedures in place to uphold and follow through on those values.

In our post-pandemic world of work, small and medium-size business leaders and their teams need to recognize that it is beneficial to conduct a review of HR policies regarding hiring and career advancement criteria. It is important to be very specific about the criteria. For example, be clear about what kind of qualifications individuals need to have, making sure to take race, sex, and age out of the equation.

The goal is to look for the best fit of relevant qualifications and what is the best addition to the company. Are they able to add something new and beneficial to the company culture?

So often, I see HR and hiring managers simply using the "good fit" paradigm. Is the person a good match for the way things already are? You want to hire people who are in alignment with the company values, but you also want to bring in people who can add to them. Who can help build, evolve, and improve the company culture to help the business grow and thrive?

One of the major impacts of the pandemic has been the necessity-driven increase in remote working models. In a study recently completed by Gartner, employees who worked remotely or on a hybrid schedule performed at equal or higher levels compared to employees who worked in the office. However, managers and senior executives described hybrid employees as underperforming compared to their in-office co-workers.

There is a bias toward the older and more familiar working models, which leads managers to be more likely to promote those who come into the office versus those who do not. Studies also show that when a hybrid option is available, women and people of color prefer to work from home when compared to white men, thus making them vulnerable to this particular bias and leading to fewer career opportunities.

As far as the discipline of employees is concerned, the first and most important component is to have policies in place that are consistent across the board. Regardless of whether you are a high performer or an employee who is struggling, a brand-new frontline worker, or in leadership, the rules and policies must apply equally to everyone.

Owners and leaders cannot be seen as being exempt. They are not above the law.

A lot of things owners used to do twenty years ago, even if they were wrong, were swept under the rug and not truly addressed. In the current culture of awareness and increased public action, such behavior is no longer being tolerated. Putting the right kinds of policies in place and training your managers and employees on proper practices makes combating ISMs a companywide part of the culture for the long term.

With regard to employee terminations, you need to have a very well-documented, well-defined process. From a performance improvement plan to giving them a verbal warning to writing them up, the process needs to be clear and fully understood. Mistakes will happen, and not everyone will live up to their full potential, but everyone needs to know and understand what will happen as a result. The consequences need to be known and consistent.

If they violate policy, they will be reprimanded, put on a performance plan, and given another opportunity before termination is decided on. Whatever the plan or policy, you must be consistent with it in every department across the company and at all levels.

Companies need to develop written policies that define rules and procedures, establish a consistent process for resolving ISM-related issues, and provide annual training programs that educate all employees on their role in preventing discrimination. It is important that HR require all employees, including ownership, to sign off that they have received the annual training, and the documentation should be stored in the employee file electronically.

As we said at the start of this chapter, we all have biases. They are based on natural impulses, but it is up to us to make sure we are aware of them and that we check them before a meeting or interview. We need to be open to building relationships with those who are different from us. We must do so not simply to be in compliance with anti-discrimination statutes but to help our companies grow into the strongest and healthiest businesses they can be.

Create forums or small groups, engage in open dialogue, and use apps to create an environment where it is safe to talk about one's views and ideas as well as any concerns or encounters with ISMs. Letting people discuss and comment on what they are experiencing allows for open and honest communication with all levels, which is very beneficial for the entire company.

A person's self-worth is greatly impacted by the experiences they have and the relationships they build over time. Look for ways to promote getting employees engaged outside of the work environment and serving the community. Getting involved with charitable organizations, for example, and doing good for the community outside of the workplace will promote personal relationships and improve the overall connection to society at large.

Ultimately, the goal is to create an environment where everyone that works at the company feels safe so they can bring the best version of themselves to work every day. Enable them to feel valued, engaged, listened to, and understood. Doing so promotes a healthy organization and a better financial performance for the company in the long run.

If you would like more information on the ISMs and how they can affect your company, I suggest that you take our free assessment at www.chuckcooper.info, which will show you what areas need improvement.

Key Takeaways

- Recognize that we all have biases based on our life experiences.

- Reading and developing your Emotional Intelligence will help you become aware of biases and become a more effective leader.

- To combat ISMs within your organization requires a fully engaged leadership that does not allow discrimination to be tolerated within the company policies and procedures.

- Commit to having open, transparent conversations with your people, and schedule small group sessions to allow for discussions on discriminatory topics and how those issues were dealt with.

Chapter 8: Communication Within the Workplace

"The art of communication is the language of leadership."
James Humes

I had the opportunity to consult for a mid-size business, which had between 120 and 150 employees depending on the time of year. The company was in disarray. The CEO had been in his role for twenty years, but based on the company records, C-Suite positions were turning over at an average of once every eight months.

The results of our Client Discovery Meetings pointed to two prominent challenges. The first was a lack of communication and leadership from the CEO, resulting in a failure to ensure all departments of the organization worked in alignment toward a common company vision. Second, the objectives given for bonuses to sales, production, shipping, and marketing managers set them to compete against each other, which created tension and a lack of trust between the teams.

As I spoke with the department managers and their teams, the number and severity of issues continued to increase. Out of more than forty members at different levels within the business, not a single person was a fan of the company. They were collecting a decent paycheck and enjoying great company benefits but were merely going through the motions each day to do their work.

Speaking with their referenceable customers revealed that they were not raving fans either. Many felt the products and services were competitive in the market, but they were lukewarm about their purchase experiences. Their issues were not with the product but with the customer service they received, as there did not seem to be a sense of urgency in resolving customer issues.

Although there were more specific issues that needed to be addressed, the overarching problems were poor communication and misalignment. The CEO was the only one who could affect the required changes, but I knew it was going to be a challenge to make any progress, as he was quick to point fingers at everyone except himself.

During the meeting to present our findings, the CEO was very closed off. He sat arms crossed, looking out the office window and cursing as he blamed the manager of each team where the issue existed. As we were finishing the list of issues identified during our Discovery meetings, he jumped up and declared the meeting over.

I tried to push for clarity regarding the next steps and timelines but received nothing definitive. As I left the office and walked to my car, I had the sense I was missing something significant but could not put a specific name to it, and I was not sure if I would get a chance to speak to the CEO again.

While reviewing my notes from the interviews, I saw it mentioned in multiple conversations that the CEO always arrived at the office early in the morning. In many cases, he was in the office at 4:30 a.m. I decided to take a gamble and attempt to meet with him by being in the company parking lot the next morning when he arrived.

It was a two-hour drive to get there, but I was able to be in the client parking lot just prior to the CEO's arrival. When I met him at the office door, he was quick to question my sanity and suggested I had only shown up to collect my consulting fee.

As we sat down in the office, I said I was not going to bill them for the work we had done, but I did have a favor to ask. I wanted the opportunity to do one final interview, with permission to dig into everything related to his work at the company and touch on his personal life. He was reluctant, but he agreed.

It was a fascinating four hours. He said that no one had ever done anything quite as stupid as I had, arriving at

such a crazy time to meet him. However, he was grateful
that I had done so and commented that he felt a sense of
relief after our interview. He shared with me some health
challenges he had faced and overcome, his struggles with
an adult child, and the impact the relationship with them
had on his marriage.

As we concluded over breakfast, I was able to better
understand the vision and mission he had for the company
when he started it and how the emotional toll of watching
it all decline over the last five years had impacted him.

One of the ideas we talked about at great length was
bringing in a new person to serve as the COO. Specifically,
someone empowered to make changes in how the
company was aligned and to the personnel they currently
had. Over the following six months, a COO was brought
onboard.

They took the first three months to get a full
understanding of the operation and personnel. Then they
developed a plan on how to implement the proposed
restructure. We were able to work closely with the
leadership team to create processes that aligned employees
with department objectives, which were tied into the
corporate vision and mission.

Communications were streamlined by establishing
quick leadership meetings each morning that discussed the

important tasks for the day, addressed any department-related questions, and focused on a company value each week. Leadership was realigned, so there were consistent goals supporting sales and marketing, as well as production and shipping.

With these changes, the silos between the departments were removed, and department managers reported directly to the COO. Communication improved, collaboration began to take place, trust was re-established, and teams were now working toward common goals.

Twelve months after the COO arrived, the CEO was a completely different person. He was more engaging and back to enjoying his work. The company was running more effectively, turnover was reduced significantly, employees were happier, and the business was performing better financially. The clear, concise, and consistent communication and the realignment of leadership aligning their mission with companywide goals led to a complete turnaround within the company.

How Do Gaps in Communication Form Between Employers and Employees?

Communication is the glue that holds a business together, but there are several factors that can cause that communication to break down. The biggest one is a lack of transparency and trust between management and employees. When this happens, staff become anxious and interpret every situation through an assumption of the worst-case scenario.

According to a recent McKinsey study, an employee's relationship with their manager is the top factor in an employee's level of job satisfaction. For most of us, a strained relationship at work will often carry over to our personal relationships, as we spend more time with our co-workers than anyone else in our life. Poor communication leads to added stress, heightened sensitivity, and a lack of joy and happiness in all aspects of our lives.

If management simply gives orders and the employees are expected to obediently carry them out, the culture within the company oozes fear and intimidation. There is no opportunity for two-way communication and no space to speak with or listen to others. You cannot effectively engage with someone if you are not listening to them and are likely to make assumptions about their needs based on your personal perceptions rather than on the reality of their experiences.

Leadership within small and medium-size companies will often utilize a command-and-control management style with strictly one-way communication from the top down through the organization. In addition, employers usually have an individual that serves as a supervisor. All communication goes through that individual who filters the information they receive through their own perceptions and assumptions before communicating the filtered message to the employees. This process creates the potential for a completely different message than the one originally intended.

Depending on the type of business, employees and management may work from different locations or on different schedules, creating a chasm that prevents direct one-to-one communication. The parties defer to email, voicemail, or text only, which can easily lead to misunderstandings or misinterpretation.

In some cases, the communication gap is caused by a difference in cultural barriers. We often think that cultural gaps only occur in international relationships, but the gap can just as easily happen regionally between neighbors. Both parties might come from the United States, but failure to recognize cultural differences can offend the other person, thus leading to a breakdown in communication.

Communication is the glue that holds a company together. If employees do not think they have a voice, they will feel they are not trusted, respected, or valued. This leads to feelings of distrust, dissatisfaction, and anxiety. Our minds naturally jump to the negative when there is poor communication. Anxiety, doubt, and uncertainty begin to dominate our thoughts, and this affects employee morale, decreases productivity, and increases employee turnover.

The cost of replacing an employee can range from one-half to two times the employee's annual salary. Thus, the cost of replacing an employee who is making $50,000 a year could be between $25,000 and $100,000. An increased rate of employee turnover can have a significant impact on a company's survival.

How to Create Good Communication Within a Company

Helping a company thrive requires leadership that makes communication a part of the company's DNA. The moment communication starts to break down, all other aspects of company functioning begin to weaken as well. Companies that have good communication have leadership that exercises these seven qualities:

1. They are good listeners; they ask questions as they seek to understand before being understood.

2. They model authenticity and are transparent with their people.

3. All communications are clear and concise.

4. They are present in the moment when interacting with people.

5. In meetings, distractions are minimized by turning off email and cellphones to make the person speaking feel what they are saying is important and they are being heard.

6. They lead by example, striving to embody the values and habits they wish to see their employees develop.

7. They are respectful of an employee's personal time by not emailing, calling, or texting them when they are no longer on the clock.

When COVID-19 hit the U.S. and the world, resulting in shutdowns and other large-scale disruptions to our lives, we were all on edge. There were so many unknowns facing us every way we turned. The pressure gauge for emotions like anxiety, fear, and uncertainty was constantly in the danger zone without any clear indication of when it would pass or when the lives we recognized might return. We all struggled to have accurate information, but the scientific community was learning and figuring things out in real-time. The data changed day by day and, in many cases, hour by hour.

Employees were craving updates from their leaders, who were only able to provide what was available at that time. New information offered comfort that we were not in this alone, that there were people working on the problem and making progress towards piecing the puzzle together.

The companies that survived and began to thrive quickly were the ones with leadership that focused on communicating with their people immediately. They provided daily updates on what management was thinking, planning, and preparing in order to stabilize the company. These regular communications offered a sense of clarity and reassurance that leadership was engaged. People could feel comfortable caring for their families, knowing their jobs were safe.

Over the past three years, company management has searched for ways to become more effective and efficient with organizational and staff meetings. Two practices that have been productive are the scheduling of regular leadership calls and minimizing the number of staff meetings.

Leadership calls are used to sync up all departments so that consistent messaging can be provided throughout the company and departmental issues are addressed with clarity. Minimizing the number of staff meetings and keeping them short and on topic gives employees more time to get their work completed.

The effective use of technology creates efficiency within a company or organization. Using instant messaging apps such as Slack to quickly respond to an employee's question enhances the quality of communications and increases the sense of being part of a team. It also displays respect for the employee's time and shows they are being heard by leadership.

The result is a team that has consistent messaging, is actively engaged, and is in a positive frame of mind, which leads to a unified and highly productive workforce of fulfilled employees.

An important part of working collaboratively and building community is creating lanes for communication to flow from the top-down and from the bottom-up throughout the organization. One challenge that many businesses have is providing safe and effective pathways for employees to bring problems or negative issues to the top leadership without fear of reprimand or retaliation.

In his book, *Remote Work*, Chris Dyer described how helpful it was to have employees practice giving him the bad news. Even when the problem was fictitious, some people struggled. However, by modeling a constructive approach during the role play, Chris was able to demonstrate to them that the emphasis would always be on creating solutions and not on pointing fingers.

As leaders, we need to keep the focus on the person. Often, the problem or business challenge gets resolved as a by-product of conversations between team members. Communication is the glue that holds a company together; it provides guidance, a reassuring sense of safety, and fosters feelings of belonging to a team and having a purpose for the work they are doing.

Key Takeaways

- Communication means asking questions and being an active listener.

- Use technology such as Slack or Teams to support your communications.

- Do your people feel comfortable bringing you bad news? It is important to have a process that allows them to bring issues to you as their leader so that they know the focus is on finding the solution and not on them.

- When leadership gives their people a voice, they recognize that they are trusted, respected, and valued.

Unprecedented

Chapter 9: Changing the Company Culture

"Corporate culture matters. How management chooses to treat its people impacts everything for better or for worse."
Simon Sinek

Henry had a decision to make and one that he knew was going to be difficult. A company that was deeply in trouble had offered him the CEO position. They were very clear with him that they were bringing him in to revamp the company and take it from a toxic place to work to a great one.

Henry loved challenges, but this one…

He asked the current management if he could take a walk around the place alone. As he did, he saw two things – dejected employees who were still doing their jobs to the best of their ability. He could tell that they love what they do but no longer who they do it for. He also saw the toxic management. He walked into one of the rooms to check it out and came into the middle of one of the managers tearing down an employee in front of everyone else. The manager glared at him and told him to get out.

As Henry walked out of the room, the decision was made. He had to do something to turn the company around. He headed back to talk to the management and tell them that he accepted.

One of the first things Henry did was to create several small focus groups to listen to the employees that were still working there. As expected, the employees were vocal about the previous leadership, the working conditions, and the negative environment. This gave him the information he needed to begin formulating a plan to turn around the operations.

There were several issues that were expected and some surprises too. After the first six months, Henry had replaced the CFO, COO, and HR Manager. He brought in a Business Consultant to assist with the turnaround, including the company's new vision, mission, and values. As part of this process, they included groups of employees, mid-level managers, and the executive team. The consultant served as the facilitator for the meetings, and they worked with the executive team to begin executing the turnaround in operations, including sales, marketing, and production.

In the first year, a new rhythm of communication was established, the executive team was able to speak with key employees who had left about their reasoning for departing, and as the issues were addressed, some of the key employees returned to leadership roles to help manage departments that they were familiar with. They were then able to build relationships and trust to the point that the leadership team was able to create strategic plans that were aligned with company goals, and the leaders were empowered to carry out their mission.

This empowerment allowed leaders to mold their teams, including replacing a few and coaching others to develop their skillset. The managers were initially held accountable for the health of their team, including training, development, and alignment with the core values of the company. In the first nine months, the company's year-over-year sales remained flat; however, there was significant progress being made with the alignment of departments, people, and new processes.

At the end of the first year, the new culture was built on trust, respect, and transparent communication, and the organization was growing in revenue and headcount. Even with everything going on in the world, the company had one of its best years ever.

What Is Company Culture?

Company culture refers to the values and behaviors that determine how a company's people and management interact with one another, how the organization makes decisions, and how they handle outside business transactions. For small and medium-sized companies, culture is a business's attitude, values, traditions, beliefs, behaviors, and goals that are a part of the company's DNA, from the executive management to the newest hired employee.

This has become a key differentiator in the marketplace. In the past, companies set themselves apart from their competitors either through unique characteristics of the products or services they provided or through competitive prices.

Much of this has been commoditized over the years, which has shifted the focus to a company's culture. People's experience interacting with the business has become just as, if not more, important than their experience of the product they are purchasing. This has become one of the primary factors that employees consider when deciding whether to remain with a company.

There are plenty of places for people to get things. They are now prioritizing their experience of the process. The quality of the process depends on the energy and behavior of your people. Your people (your company's greatest asset) are your most powerful differentiator.

The ideal company culture is one that projects a strong, clear vision and gives employees a sense of purpose in their work. It is a motivational force for both management and employees. As they begin to internalize the behaviors and values of the organization, they start to feel confident in the work they are doing. When your people have self-confidence, trust develops, and they feel empowered and fulfilled.

Company culture thrives on trust between the organization and its people. This means knowing what to do and also understanding how and why to do it. This trust provides the alignment of personal goals with the company vision and allows everyone to work together. It sets the tone for the entire organization and is a key driver of a company's success.

Company Culture Starts from the CEO Down

As leaders, we need to be intentional and purposeful in how we design the culture of our company. Leaving it to chance is not a best practice, as it traps you in a purely reactionary mode, which makes you vulnerable to being caught unprepared. Effective leaders make creating a culture that is purposeful and mission-centered a top priority from the very start.

The CEO is responsible for establishing the company culture. They set the tone and speak with the greatest passion and conviction. They have the most clarity about what they want the culture and mission of the organization to be, as well as the strategies they envision for achieving the short and long-term goals. They carry significant influence within the company and are the face of the organization to the community and all stakeholders.

CEOs ultimately shape and lead their culture by building high-performing organizations and by aligning their people, customers, suppliers, stakeholders, and shareholders with mutually beneficial objectives.

It is also important to remember that the people in the organization have an important role in shaping and carrying out a company's vision and culture. The question that employees are asked most often about their place of work is, "What is it like to work at this company?" Their response gives a clear picture of what kind of a culture they feel they are a part of.

As David Friedman says in his book, *Culture by Design,* when asking CEOs about the importance of culture, most will rank it a 4 on a scale of 1–5. However, when those same CEOs are asked if they have a documented plan for intentionally driving the culture of their company, typically, only a couple will raise their hand.

When leadership conducts Strategic Business Planning meetings for the upcoming year, they usually have detailed presentations on sales, marketing, and financial budgets, yet there is often little to nothing about the one thing that acts as the greatest differentiator: the company's culture and its people.

How to Create a Company Mission and Value Statement

The creation of a company mission statement and company values begins with the CEO and often includes additional members of the C-Suite. If the company is smaller, then the business owner should form an executive or advisory team to be a part of the process.

These sessions need to be held away from the office. They must be free from distractions and consist of a group and facilitator asking questions and helping everyone share ideas such as the following:

- Who are we?
- Why does the organization exist?
- The mission statement needs to inspire, include the company's purpose, and reveal the values of the company.
- All members need to share thoughts and words.
- All ideas need to be collected and considered.
- Use those words to write the statement.
- Examine the statement and ask if this is reflective of the organization.

- Read it out loud and see if everyone agrees it is reflective of why the organization exists.

- Ask everyone if they agree with the statement or what modifications are needed.

We have seen many cases where a company creates a list of between ten and twelve different core values, but when asked, the employees and leadership do not remember them. Such a list might look great on the wall, but if only a small percentage of the people, including management, embody them consistently, it creates confusion and a lack of trust inside the organization and with your outside stakeholders.

A great resource, I highly recommend the book *Culture by Design* by David J. Friedman. The author does a great job of walking the reader through the process of creating mission and vision statements, company values and helping to understand how these items impact a company's culture.

After the mission statement is written, the group should work together to identify clear actions that will support the values of the organization. Aim for a list of three to five values that best represent your organization. Then, create a list of three to five actions that support each of the values. In many cases, the values selected can have different meanings to different people, which is why it is important the actions be clear and concrete to ensure the goal and meaning are understood.

Some examples of a well thought out mission statement are:

- LinkedIn: "To connect the world's professionals to make them more productive and successful."

- Southwest Airlines: "The mission of Southwest Airlines is dedication to the highest quality of customer service delivered with a sense of warmth, friendliness, individual pride, and company spirit."

- Microsoft: "Our mission is to empower every person and every organization on the planet to achieve more."

A few examples of poorly written mission statements (in my opinion) are:

- Albertsons: "To create a shopping experience that pleases our customers; a workplace that creates opportunities and a great working environment for our associates; and a business that achieves financial success." [They do not identify what business they are actually in.]

- Sony: "To be a company that inspires and fulfills your curiosity." [It is unhelpfully vague.]

- MoMA: "To collect, preserve, study, exhibit, and stimulate appreciation for and advance knowledge of works of art that collectively represent the broadest spectrum of human achievement at the highest level of quality, all in the service of the public and in accordance with the highest professional standards." [The mission cannot be to do everything.]

How to Instill Values into Your Company

Leadership must create a strategic plan for how they are going to work on the company culture throughout the year. Identify and have absolute clarity about the behaviors you want your people to have. For example:

1. Be clear on expectations.

2. Honor your word or commitment.

3. Always do what is in the client's best interest.

Build a curriculum to teach employees your culture. This provides a tool to ensure that what is being taught across all departments (including as part of new employee orientation) is consistent with the company's mission and values.

Be careful when selecting who will be on your team. Your mission and values guide your company, so it is crucial that the people you bring into that company are onboard and consistent with that vision. Build the topic of culture into your onboarding process. New employees must be taught this culture, and it should be taught by the CEO or the person with the highest ranking at that location. Communicate your culture throughout the entire organization. Managers and leaders need to serve as culture coaches. Leaders lead by example.

As we meet and spend time with leadership teams, we get a sense of what the company's culture is very quickly. People's energy is easy to read, from the attitude an employee has to the way managers communicate with their teams. You can also tell when people are genuinely engaged or are just going through the motions to get their work completed and collect a paycheck.

The Importance of Managing 1–1 Instead of 1–Team

For years, we have focused on how we can do tasks quicker as our to-do list continues growing. As managers, our work became more about completing a checklist than it did about tending to our people. As we look back, it is easy to see why many workers lost motivation and did not feel fulfilled in the work they were doing.

For so many of us, our identity is tied up in our careers and the work we do. If we are not being successful at work, it flows into all aspects of our lives, affecting how we perceive the quality of our home life and our life's purpose.

Due to COVID-19, everything in our personal and professional lives was turned upside down. However, it did give us time to think and reflect on life. Some people spent the time waiting and hoping life would return to the way it used to be. Others saw the pandemic as a time to reassess and elected to move forward with the idea of creating a new normal for their life.

This included determining what their personal mission, vision, and values were (or what they wanted them to be). Then, through this realignment, people were making changes in how they lived and why they worked.

This is why leaders need to become students of emotional intelligence and develop the ability to be agile in how they approach challenges and interact with people. No longer does one size fit all, if it ever truly did. We are all individuals, and we have unique motivators—intrinsic and extrinsic—so it is imperative that leaders and managers bring the human aspect back to the work that they do.

Taking care of your people and creating a work environment that inspires employees to bring the best version of themselves to work every day is critical to a company's success. Get to know each member on your team personally in order to fully understand what is important to them, how they are motivated, and recognize how their personal mission or passions align with that of the company.

Even though this involves blurring the lines of our personal and work lives to a degree, a deeper relationship is formed, and trust is built, which is good! Rather than make assumptions, managers can better understand their people in order to recognize when they become overloaded or when they are being fulfilled and have additional bandwidth to give more to their work.

Transitioning Leadership to a Coach/Mentor Model

When we look at how work has changed since COVID-19, as well as what the future of work is projected to be, and then overlay that with the needs and expectations of younger generations, there are ample reasons why the role of a manager needs to become more that of a coach toward their team members.

Research shows that effective coaching in the workplace leads to better engagement, higher productivity, and enhanced customer service. It also helps employees improve performance, overcome challenges, reach aspirational goals, and build self-confidence. According to *Harvard Business Review*, an effective manager coaches and asks questions instead of providing answers, supports employees instead of judging them, and facilitates their development instead of dictating what has to be done.

This transition may require additional training and development to help managers to evolve and enhance their people skills. In some situations, although a manager has been in their position for several years and has served a company well, this does not mean they will be fully prepared to take on a more coach-style role going forward. One of the key indicators to show if a manager will make a good coach is how coachable and open to professional development they are.

To adapt to all the changes and evolutions in the workplace, executives and managers need to have the mindset of a perpetual student, that is, someone who is always learning, wanting to grow, remaining curious, and seeking a better perspective.

Having a mentor program within your organization at all levels can be incredibly valuable. Despite 76 percent of people claiming mentors are important, only 37 percent say they currently have one. Encouraging coaching and mentorship have proven to help retain skilled and happy employees. Plus, the guidance from a coach and mentor can help your employees evolve into strong leaders themselves.

Should Annual Reviews Continue to Be Performed?

First, let us look at the overall effectiveness of annual reviews. Our experience when talking with HR managers and business owners is that performance reviews are a pain for everyone involved. In many cases, there is little to no pre-planning done by the manager prior to the actual review being conducted, which leads to an awkward exchange. The manager is often in a hurry to complete it, and the conclusions drawn are mostly subjective rather than based on facts.

How does that help a company and its people? The answer is it does not.

Most questions on performance review documents are not relevant to the employee's actual performance or what they have worked on over the previous twelve months. In essence, the discussion surrounding performance reviews is spent looking back at particular situations that happened six to twelve months prior without any attempt at coaching and improvement.

In our estimation, annual performance reviews should be replaced. There are several alternatives that companies are trying as they seek to find the model that works best for them.

The first option is to schedule more frequent reviews, such as once per quarter or even semi-annually. However, these do not really address the core issues that companies are struggling with when conducting annual reviews. Too much of the time is still spent doing administrative work, and the focus continues to look back instead of moving forward.

Next is to consider implementing a review process where the focus turns to accomplishments and goals, making it easier for the manager or coach to quantify and reduce the risk of subjectivity. This is a model that small and medium-size companies are transitioning to as they are watching how performance and productivity are affected when employees work remotely or within a hybrid model versus those who work in the office.

If you want your performance reviews to be effective, it is going to require the following:

1. Managers must commit to extensive preparation before conducting their reviews.

2. Be clear with your communication.

3. Be specific about the attainable goals.

4. Communicate the "why" of the employees' work and how their efforts contribute to the success of the company.

5. Utilize 360-degree feedback.

We recommend that employers replace annual reviews with regular check-ins and ongoing feedback. There must be consistent follow-up between the manager and employee to ensure goals are being met and to also provide opportunities for feedback.

This allows for two-way communication, for coaches to give praise when performance is going well, and it also builds relationships that allow for challenging conversations when coaching and correction are needed. The latter should occur at a time when the facts are clear in both the employee and coach's minds. In short, having lots of little conversations over time can lead to big results.

How Should Performance Now Be Measured?

In the past, we have measured performance based on employee self-evaluation, manager evaluation, and how the employee performed based on company metrics. Performance goals must clearly define the expected end results to be accomplished.

To the extent possible, goals should have a direct link to organizational success factors, and goals should be difficult yet achievable to motivate performance. Performance goals should be created through collaboration between the employee and their manager.

The top five skills an employee's performance should measure are:

1. Quality of work
2. Speed
3. Dependability
4. Adherence to company values
5. Teamwork

Performance management is about helping the company achieve its mission and vision by working to improve the staff and increase their effectiveness. Areas that are important to this process are:

1. Establishing clear expectations
2. The providing of continuous feedback
3. Training and development programs to help employees learn and grow
4. Recognizing employee performance that meets and exceeds goals

The expectations that are established should be objective, monitored regularly, and easy to track for both the employees and their managers or coaches.

All of this combined together will help to create a company culture that is attractive not only to the employees but also to vendors and the clients they serve.

We are almost there. In the next chapter, we will sum it all up and give you an action plan moving forward.

Key Takeaways

- How to build a culture where people feel valued: https://whitewaterconsulting.net/creating-a-culture-where-people-feel-valued/.

- The CEO is responsible for the company culture. The people within the organization have an important role in shaping and carrying out the values and the culture.

- Incorporate the topic of culture into your annual planning meeting, and develop a strategy for how you are going to make your culture better in the year ahead.

Chapter 10: The Next Step is Yours

"Knowing is not enough! You must take action."
Tony Robbins

Now we have reached the final and most important stage of the journey: taking action. We have covered the major topics with regard to building and sustaining a thriving company culture, but the information is only as useful as the actions that follow. Once the information has been explored, it is time to put it into practice.

Whether you are starting a new business, or your company has been up and running for years, every day is a chance to take decisive action toward making your company and yourself successful. This book was written specifically to try and help you figure out what moves you need to make.

Leadership

Trust is an asset of immeasurable value. Achieving trust with your people requires building strong relationships by being transparent, authentic, and available.

Even before the pandemic, leadership models were shifting away from top-down command structures, and the past two years have added rocket fuel to those changes. Moving forward, the focus of leadership must be on creating a company culture and environment that enables employees to bring the best versions of themselves to work every day. Building trust and respect with all of the people across your company requires:

- Being authentic, transparent, and vulnerable with your people.

- Communicating clearly, concisely, and consistently.

- Listening intently and always seeking to understand.

- Strengthening your emotional intelligence to be agile and adaptable.

- Developing a collaborative management style.

- Showing gratitude to your people.

- Establishing a culture of inclusion, diversity, and respectful questioning, yet expecting unity once the decision is made.

Effective leadership means being clear about your purpose as an individual and as a company. Exceptional leadership means authentically living the values of your organization at all times and on all levels because your people are watching.

Being a leader does not mean that you have to go it alone, however. It can get lonely at the top. When difficult challenges arise, do not be afraid to ask for help. We strongly encourage becoming a part of a CEO peer group such as Vistage and C12. They have proven to be extremely valuable to our clients during periods of growth, as well as throughout all the chaos caused by COVID-19.

If you do not have the resources to invest in a CEO peer group, then we recommend creating your own board of advisors that includes your executive management team and, possibly, a couple of outside resources in whom you have full confidence and trust. Such groups will serve you best if you commit to transparency, authenticity, and confidentiality. As we have mentioned throughout this book, the journey of an entrepreneur and executive should not be made alone. We all have times when we need support, encouragement, and some guardrails.

Understanding Generational Needs

Creating an environment where everyone feels valued requires an understanding of the common perspectives and approaches of each generation and seeking out the common ground between them. Remember, one size does not fit all. To be successful, modern leaders must be fluent in the various needs of different generations and be adaptable in their perspectives and approaches in order to meet them. From knowledge and wisdom gained through real life experience to the strength and energy of youth to the understanding of technology, everyone brings value to the team.

Communication plays an important role in creating trust, respect, and valuing of all generations. Creating opportunities that promote team building outside of work is a great way to build connections. Game nights, virtual tastings, tailgating before the game, book clubs, or holiday parties— are all opportunities to boost morale and strengthen personal relationships between colleagues.

People, regardless of generation, want to believe the work they are doing is having a meaningful and positive impact on their community and on society. Leaders wanting to meet their employees' needs must do everything they can to let them know they are appreciated, are being heard, and are respected. People are every company's greatest asset!

HR Best Practices

Determining the role that HR is going to play in your start-up is a key component in your business plan, as it will set the tone for how leadership is going to view your people. HR best practices help leadership focus on the needs of the organization through providing proper practices, procedures, and infrastructure to support and develop their employees. This includes talent acquisition and retention, providing training and development to help their team grow, and providing the tools and skills needed to fulfill the vision of the organization.

Conducting regularly scheduled audits is a crucial way to mitigate the liability of being an employer by helping to ensure the company's policies, procedures, and documents remain in compliance. This includes, for example, how employee I9 forms and supporting documentation are managed. We strongly recommend that these documents be stored in a separate file from the employee file. Ideally, they should be stored electronically for security purposes and for ease of access. A valuable resource to help with this can be found at www.uscis.gov.

With The Great Resignation or The Reshuffling of the Workforce, the talent selection process and staff retention strategies around salaries and promotions are real hot-button issues for companies of all sizes. In order to avoid the types of discrimination that we discussed in Chapter 7; it is important to consistently audit these areas. Employers must now consider remote and hybrid workers and how they will be factored into the selection and promotion processes.

Outsourcing

Outsourcing is an extremely valuable option for an entrepreneur. Until you have been through the launch and start-up phase of a small business, it is hard to comprehend how overwhelming it can be to try and manage every aspect of the company. Thus, view HR as a strategic resource for your company, and seek out the resources to build the foundation proactively. It requires a financial investment, but the cost of waiting and operating reactively will cost significantly more.

We encourage leaders of small and mid-size companies to identify the areas they have expertise in and consider outsourcing areas like HR. This way, leadership can stay focused on growing revenues, controlling expenses, and coaching their people. Based on twenty-five years of experience, we believe that HR outsourcing serves small and mid-size companies extremely well. The question for you as the leader is, which outsourcing model will serve you the best: PEO or ASO?

As you work through the decision-making process, it is important to understand that all PEOs are different. You will see the differences in the way the sales rep presents the proposal, pricing, technology platform, breadth of services, and service delivery capabilities. Over the years, I have heard repeatedly from prospective clients that after conducting an in-depth evaluation of HR outsourcing providers, they felt overwhelmed and found it challenging to select a PEO they were confident with.

To hear about business owners investing their time and resources in an evaluation process only to wind up without any clarity and peace of mind at the conclusion is heartbreaking. I launched White Water Consulting, which is a business consulting practice that specializes in HR for small and mid-size companies, as a way to solve this problem.

We use our experience and relationships within the HR industry to educate our clients on the options. Then, we manage the evaluation process so that when our clients are ready to decide on a provider, they can do so with confidence and clear understanding.

Compliance

HR compliance is not a nice-to-have; it is a *must*-have. Often, business owners cite a lack of time and financial resources as reasons their business is not in compliance. These responses are not sufficient when you consider the impact on the integrity of your company, your employees, and your stakeholders. The investigators with the Department of Revenue, EEOC, and OSHA (Occupational

Safety and Health Administration) will not find the responses sufficient either.

A couple of years after we purchased our manufacturing plant in northern Illinois, I remember the day when a gentleman from the OSHA walked into my office, introduced himself, and said that I would need to spend the day with him. He asked for a tour of the facility, to speak with our plant managers, and had an extensive list of documents he needed to review as part of an audit. I proceeded to put my ignorance on display, stating that the day was not good as we were extremely busy, and he would need to call and schedule an appointment.

Over the next two days, the audit generated a list of around twenty different violations that we needed to address and thousands of dollars in fines. Thus, I learned the impact of waiting until there was a storm before addressing the issue versus being proactive and having policies, procedures, and documentation completed as part of our standard process.

Not only could we have saved time and resources by having complied with OSHA guidelines before the official audit, but the situation also damaged the trust and respect our employees felt for the company leadership. When you violate a person's trust, it takes a significant amount of work to earn it back, and you forfeit the right to determine when or if the trust can be regained.

Dealing With ISMs

We all have our own inherent biases. It is part of human nature. Effective leaders do everything they can to prevent those biases from negatively influencing the functioning of their businesses. A company's culture is set by its leader. It, therefore, needs to be a personal mission of the leader to not allow ISMs to be present in the company policies and procedures. You want to ensure you are communicating the message that the organization is going to treat everyone fairly regardless of age, gender, sex, or race.

Develop written policies that define rules and procedures, establish a consistent process for resolving ISM-related issues, and instate annual training programs for all employees to help prevent discrimination. Require all employees, including ownership, to receive that annual training and document it in their employee file.

The best way to combat bias and discrimination is by being open to building relationships with those who are different from us. Establish forums or small groups, have open dialogue, and use apps to create an environment where it is safe to talk about views, ideas, and concerns. Letting people share what they are experiencing allows for open and honest communication, which benefits the entire company.

The aim is for a workplace where everyone feels safe so they can bring the best version of themselves daily. Helping them to feel happy, engaged, listened to, and understood promotes a healthy organization and better financial performance for the company in the long run.

Communication

Communication is the glue that holds our personal and business relationships together. Leaders must communicate clearly, regularly, and to everyone in the organization. This provides ongoing clarity and transparency, which builds trust and respect. Most people (including leaders) do not like surprises, so you must commit to keeping everyone in the organization updated. Make sure your people hear clear and consistent messages from the CEO or a business owner. You do not have to provide all the details, but it is important you give enough information to promote understanding.

Stay attuned to topics such as race relations, discrimination, and mental health by holding small group meetings where leaders and employees come together to discuss the issues. It provides everyone with the ability to have a voice and creates psychological safety throughout the organization. Being able to ask questions and hear differing perspectives provides a great opportunity for everyone involved to be seen and heard, which builds a strong bond of community, loyalty, and trust.

Communication with stakeholders is important as well. Building relationships with suppliers, customers, business partners, investors, and the local community can lead to a stronger connection with your company. By setting up forums for interaction and inviting feedback, you can gain a better understanding of your stakeholders' interests and attitudes, thus enabling you to fine-tune your communications. Utilizing social media can also spread your message further through your stakeholders' extended networks.

Company Culture

A company's culture starts at the top and flows down through the organization. Including culture as part of your strategic planning for the year and creating a documented plan for how you will intentionally drive your company's culture going forward is a vital component of building and sustaining a strong and thriving organization.

Being crystal clear about your company's mission, vision, and values is important as they all tie into the culture that you build. A company's culture is a powerful way to differentiate itself from its competitors. Although that culture is set by the CEO, the employees play a major role in shaping and carrying it out. Whether you have a good culture, or a world-class culture depends on all of you.

It Is Time to Take Action

To all the entrepreneurs, this book was written with you in mind. I believe that entrepreneurship in the U.S. is one of the greatest differentiators we have as a country. My hope is that this book will encourage you to take a calculated risk and launch your business. Do not let fear and uncertainty keep you from taking that all-important first step.

Live your life in a way that enables you to say, "I am glad I did," rather than "I wish I would have." Your journey as an entrepreneur will be an inspiration to your family, friends, future employees, and customers. Be sure to document the wins, challenges, and lessons learned; then, pass it all on when you mentor the next generation of entrepreneurs.

I want to thank you for investing the time to read **UNPRECEDENTED: *Building a Multi-Generational Business on Trust, Respect, and the Valuing of People.***

If you are a leader in your business and you have questions about challenges related to your people, I invite you to visit my website www.chuckcooper.info and complete the ten-question assessment.

Upon completion, we will benchmark your responses against other small and mid-size companies, and you will receive your overall score. We will be happy to discuss your results with you and your team during a complimentary session. As I close, I want to wish you the best in your entrepreneurial career, and I hope that this book has helped you to see the greatest value in your business—the people. If you focus on them, you will be amazed at how incredible your business can be.

Unprecedented

About the Author:
Chuck Cooper

Chuck Cooper is the Founder of White Water Consulting in Charlotte, NC. Entrepreneur, Business Consultant, Mentor, Husband, Father, and Papa are all titles that Chuck Cooper carries proudly. Chuck is blessed to be married to his wife Debbie, and they are the parents of three adult children and grandparents to ten grandchildren.

Growing up in a farming community, the son and grandson of small business owners, family and family traditions have always been an important part of life. However, it wasn't until after he went through some deep valleys on his life's journey, which caused him to become introspective that Chuck began to see his life with greater clarity. It was during these years that he was able to clarify his vision of his life's purpose and passions and establish the principles he wanted to live his life by. This led him to his ultimate mission: serving, supporting, and helping others achieve higher levels of success.

For the past twenty-six years, Chuck Cooper has committed to that mission by serving small and mid-size business owners by helping connect leadership with their people. Chuck believes that people are a company's greatest asset, which is why he is passionate about helping bridge the gap within a multi-generational workforce and building trust throughout the organization. He has found that by being authentic and transparent in his communication, he has been able to use his life experiences—the victories and the failures—to build trust with people at all levels of an organization.

His focus today is on building and expanding the legacy he will leave to his children and grandchildren. Chuck was entrusted with a rich legacy that was started by his grandparents, passed to his parents, and then on to him. His passion is to build a legacy that includes Faith, Family, and Love through the serving of others.

While specific quotes have been noted, I feel it is important to note these works that broadened my knowledge and influenced the concepts presented in this book:

- White, Dana K., *Decluttering at the Speed of Life*, 2018, W Publishing/ Thomas Nelson Ltd.
- Friedman, David J., *Culture By Design*, 2018, Infinity Publishing.
- Dyer, Chris & Shepherd, Kim, *Remote Work*, 2021, Kogan Page
- Sarvadi, Paul, *Take Care of your People*, 2019, Forbes Books
- White, Dana K., "Winning the Battle with STUFF", *Good Housekeeping*, Hearst Media, Oct.23, 2017

Unprecedented